The 'Lost'

Village of Lawers

by

Mark Bridgeman

Originally published in 2020 by
Mark Bridgeman

Copyright © Mark Bridgeman, 2020

This edition published by
Brindle Books Ltd
Wakefield
United Kingdom

www.brindlebooks.co.uk

The right of Mark Bridgeman to be identified
as the author of this work has been asserted
by him in accordance with theCopyright,
Design and Patent Act 1988.

All rights reserved. No part of this publication may be
reproduced, stored in a retrieval system or transmitted, in any
form or by any means, electronic, mechanical, photocopying,
recording or otherwise without the prior permission of the
Copyright holder

ISBN 978-1-915631-20-6

Lawers *proper noun. (English).* Translation (Scots. Gaelic) **'Labhuir'.** Pronounced (Scots. Gaelic) *'loo-aahhs'*. Meaning – *'The Noisy One'*. Name of an abandoned village on Lochtayside, Perthshire. The name derives from the loud sound of water in the burn running from Ben Lawers into Loch Tay.

taibhsear *noun.* (*plural* **taibhsearan**) (pronounced **tive'sher**). English literal translation – **'ghost seer'**. A title given to a person who possesses the gift of *dà-shealladah* (second sight), a foreteller, seer, soothsayer, prophet. Traditionally, an individual would not name themselves a *Taibhsear*; instead, the title would be a mark of reverence, respect, or even fear, earned within the community. A *Taibhsear*, it was believed could bridge the divide between the world of the living and the 'Otherworld' of the dead. With this unique capability came visions, such as revelations of future events, or premonitions of death.

The 'Lost' Village of Lawers

A journey from Kenmore, in Perthshire, along the A827 towards Killin gives the driver unrivalled views of Loch Tay. As the road gradually ascends one reaches the tiny village of Lawers, a scattered collection of cottages, farms, and a hotel. Yet this small community is not the original village given the name Lawers.

Originally the 'lost' and now abandoned settlement of Lawers was situated a mile down the hillside on the shores of Loch Tay. Lawers was once a flourishing and important community, whose influence would reach across the county.

This small village offered work, shelter, and education to the once larger Lochtayside population. It provided able recruits for the Perthshire Militia and was famously home to one of the most enigmatic and mysterious figures in Perthshire folklore.

So why did this once thriving centre of manufacture cease to exist and just who was the mysterious 'Lady of Lawers'?

Lawers takes its name from the Gaelic for 'the noisy one', no doubt referring to the burn that tumbles down the hillside from Ben Lawers into the loch. One of the earliest references to Lawers was recorded in 1160, when King Malcolm IV of Scotland (Gaelic: Máel Coluim mac Eanric) granted the barony of Lawers to the MacMillans of Argyllshire.

King Malcolm IV of Scotland

Once an important terminal for the ferry across the loch to Ardtalnaig, on the southern shore, the remains of the pier still protrude from the water; and are a reminder that for centuries before the steamboats, people and goods were ferried up and down the loch, some calling into Lawers on their journeys. Cattle, brought to market from the south side, would be barged across the water to Lawers. On a Sunday morning, half the congregation of Lawers church would arrive by boat from the other side of the loch. As recently as the early twentieth century the Loch Tay Steamboats stopped here on their Loch Tay excursions. Interestingly, the earliest recorded map reference to the pier refers to 'Milton Pier', however all future maps and surveys use the name 'Lawers Pier'.

Despite an Historic Scotland Preservation Order being applied to the site in 1995, the long-abandoned village has gradually decayed into an overgrown and tumbled down collection of cottages, a jetty for the Loch Tay ferries, and a church (bearing a date stone inscribed 1669). A once partly cobbled track, defined by stone dykes linked the two sides of the village (separated by a common feeding ground for animals), leading to the roaring burn that provided the village's drinking water and would eventually help power the two lint mills constructed there. An old, rickety wooden bridge, now thankfully supported by a modern iron frame beneath, crosses the burn giving access to the burial ground, known as Cladh Machuim (the burial ground of the Machuim, or the tomb of the plains), built on slightly raised ground and protected by high drystone walls. It is thought that an even older church known as the Chapel of Machuim stood here for many years before the building of Lawers Church in 1669, as foundations were discovered during excavations in the 1990s. The original Chapel of Machuim was probably razed to the ground by the Duke of Montrose in 1645. It is also believed that stones from the original Chapel were used in the construction of the new church building in 1669. The enclosed graveyard of Cladh Machuim has undoubtedly been in use for many centuries, with descendants of Lawers' residents having been buried there as recently as 2018. The old chapel and graveyard probably takes its name from the nearby farm of Machuim. Within the enclosure are several interesting gravestones, including that of a carpenter or builder, which lies recumbent midway along the northwest wall. In addition to an inscription, it features fine relief carvings of a set-square, dividers, chisel, mallet, and axe, all within a moulded border and surmounted by an angel with spread wings. To the southeast of this stone there are three roughly-hewn slabs, one of which bears the initial 'M' and the date 1786, another the initials 'W M' and (apparently) the date 1531. The third displays a possible cross, whose shaft is formed by a row of spaced dots and arms linked by a crossbar. Beside the southwest wall of the burial-ground there are three other early slabs. One has a small cross, the initial 'G' and the date 1731, the second bears a small cross at the top and the legend 'D Clerk', while the third is blank. There are also several worn slabs lying in the belt of woodland between the burial ground and the edge of the loch. Perhaps even more unmarked graves, now overgrown, lie in the fields surrounding the graveyard? It is unlikely that the original site was walled, or had a defined boundary, due to its great age.

Lastly, the font from the old church is stored in a toolshed, just outside the gate to the burial ground. It was believed to have been placed there in 1938 when the small shed was erected for the storing of tools. The huge piece of stone is probably from the original Chapel of Machuim and is believed to be at least half a millennium old.

D Clerk, gravestone

Cladh Machuim was depicted in John Farquarson's *1769 Survey of the North Side of Loch Tay*, which is stored at the National Library of Scotland, and also on the first edition of the Ordnance Survey map of Perthshire in 1867. Its spelling is sometimes recorded as Mahuim or Mahuaim of Lawers.

The *'forty-merk land'* of Lawers was one of the earliest possessions of the Glenorchy Campbells on Loch Tayside (a merk was an old Scottish silver coin and it's worth was often used to value land). The territory of Lawers was bestowed upon Sir Colin Campbell, the first laird, in 1473, by James III for Sir Colin's zeal in pursuing and bringing to justice the murderers of his grandfather, James I. The land had, prior to that, been in the possession of Thomas Chalmers, one of those originally implicated in the murder of James I – a perfect revenge for James III. Sir Colin Campbell then bequeathed the land of Lawers to John, his son by his fourth wife, Margaret Stirling, so ensuring the Lawers branch of the Clan Campbell.

The Campbells gradually acquired other lands and titles in the area. By 1587 the *Royal Roll* lists Sir John Campbell, the Laird of Lawers, as among the most important *'Landis-lords and Baillies in the Hielands and lies.'*

The Campbells constructed a small castle or tower house (similar to the keeps that once stood on Wester Ardeonaig, Finlarig and Edramuckie) close to the water's edge in Lawers sometime in the 16th century. Records show this house to have been in existence from at least 1513, and possibly earlier.

An earlier date is probable, as historians agree that from approximately 1480 until after the Scottish Reformation in 1560, very few tower houses of consequence were constructed.

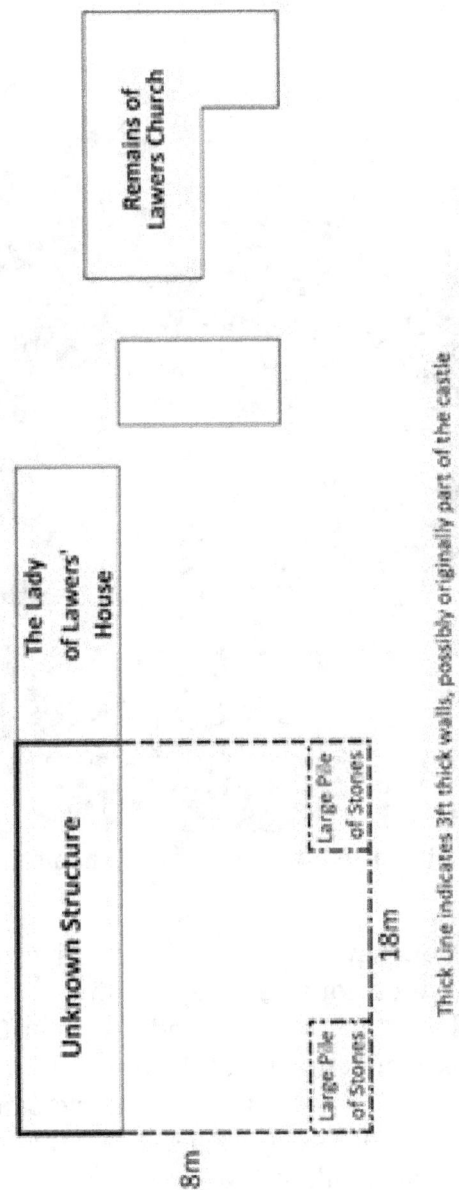

Thick Line indicates 3ft thick walls, possibly originally part of the castle
Thin line indicates 2ft thick walls, probably newer and built after the razing of the castle
Broken line indicates possible original layout of castle, suggesting an 18 square metre structure

A typical Scottish towerhouse of the period

The Castle of Lawers appears to have been a messuage (manor house estate) of some importance locally, as the estate was granted a Crown Charter, enabling legal documents to be served there. An investigation by the Ben Lawers Historic Landscape Project (1996–2005) suggested that the tower house may have been smaller than other contemporary examples, perhaps with an internal floor area of 16 square metres (whereas, for example, Elphinstone

Castle in East Lothian had an internal floor area of 25m square metres).

However, the description contained in the newly discovered story in Appendix C (see later) suggests it may have been a little larger. My measurements, taken recently at the village, seem to support the theory that the external measurements of the castle may have been 18 square metres (with an internal floor area of 16 square metre). The existence of two thicker walls, forming an 'L' shape, in one of the remaining structures may have actually been reused walls from the original castle. The two collapsed piles of large stones to the south-west and A typical Scottish tower of the period south-east of these walls also strongly suggests the square shaped outline of the castle.

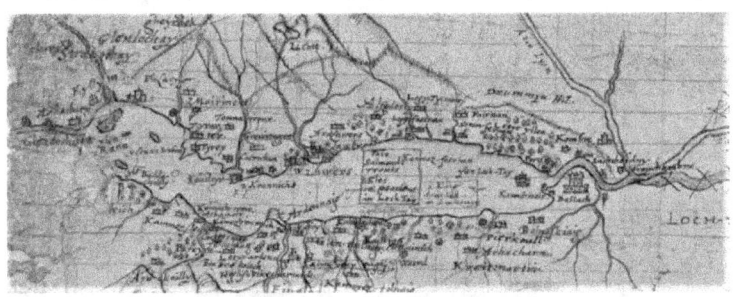

Map by Timothy Pont, c.1600, clearly showing Lawers

Around 1600 the Rev. Timothy Pont, a Scottish minister, cartographer and topographer, produced the first detailed map of Scotland. Lawers, including the castle, is clearly marked on the map, highlighting its importance, compared to nearby settlements such as Kenmore. The importance and prestige of the castle and its inhabitants was highlighted in September 1601, when the Laird of Lawers was paid the not inconsiderable sum of £1,200 by the Privvy Council in Edinburgh, to assist 'by power and force in reducing these (the Clan MacGregor) rebellious and detestable limmers to obedience and conformity to the laws'. It is difficult to place an equivalent value on this amount today, but it would certainly be in excess of £25,000.

The authorities must have found the Campbells' efforts to be money well spent, however. Later, in 1633, when an act for the further suppression of the Macgregor Clan was passed, Sir John Campbell, was appointed one of the Scottish Justices and Sheriff of Perthshire, charged with dealing with the worst lawless excesses of the clans. Charles I also appointed him Earl of Loudoun in 1633, and his younger brother succeeded him as the Laird of Lawers.

Sir John Campbell,
1st Earl of Loudoun

Nevertheless, the status and authority of the castle at Lawers seems to have lasted only a relatively short time.

James Graham, 1ˢᵗ Duke of Montrose

James Graham, the 1st Duke of Montrose, burnt down and completely destroyed the castle in 1645, during the 'War of the Three Kingdoms'. He wreaked havoc all along Lochtayside destroying many buildings, including the castle and the original chapel at Lawers.

A Scottish nobleman and soldier, James Graham supported King Charles I of England during the English Civil War. From 1644 to 1646, and again in 1650, he fought in the civil war across Scotland on behalf of the King. Many of the Clan Campbell from Lawers were killed by the Duke's men at the Battle of Inverlochy in February 1645. Despite superior numbers the Scottish parliamentary forces, under Sir Duncan Campbell, lost approximately 1,500 men.

At the Battle of Auldearn in May, 1645 – once again against the forces of Montrose - Colonel Campbell of Lawers, who had commanded the footsoldiers on the right flank at the Battle of Inverlochy, fell fighting against the Loyalists. His brother, Archibald, was also taken prisoner.

Nevertheless, the Duke of Montrose did not enjoy his victory for long. Following King Charles' defeat at the Battle of Naseby and subsequent execution, James Graham was himself captured in 1650 at the Battle of Carbisdale. He was then tried by the Scottish Parliament in Edinburgh and sentenced to death by hanging, followed by beheading and quartering. Unfortunately for the Duke, one of those sitting in judgement over him was the Chancellor of the Scottish Parliament John Campbell, 1st Earl of Loudoun, the son of Sir John Campbell of Lawers. Apparently, he took great pleasure in pronouncing the Duke's list of crimes to the court. Following the Duke's execution, his head was removed and stood on the *'prick on the highest stone of the Old Tolbooth'* outside St Giles Cathedral in Edinburgh from 1650 until the beginning of 1661.

Ruins of The Lady of Lawers' house

Following the razing of the castle at Lawers by the Duke of Montrose in 1645 the Campbells replaced the building with a less pretentious structure which would remain occupied long after the Campbells had departed. There is a firm record of the new, much smaller, dwelling

being in place by 1664; and comprising a two-storey structure with a thatched roof. It appears to be built from water worn boulders and some stonework from the original tower house. At the western end of the new two-storey structure the walls appear to be thicker, which may indicate they originally formed part of the castle.

The tumbled down structures surrounding the new house are perhaps also part of what remains from the castle. The judicious recycling of older materials and the reuse of an existing wall strongly suggests that the new dwelling was constructed on a tighter budget which did not allow for the importation of any, more expensive, raw materials.

How The Lady of Lawers might have appeared in typical Highland dress of the mid-17th Century.

Its existence is also confirmed in the Perth County Records of 1752. Sir James Campbell was left in great debt following the destruction of the castle by the Duke of Montrose, and the much smaller home he constructed may well have been based on financial necessity rather than a desire to be less conspicuous.

Census records show that it was lived in by the tenants of Milton of Lawers Farm until the last decade of the 19th century. Although conditions must have been difficult for these final tenants, as the structure is listed as a 'roofless ruin' in the Ordnance Survey of 1892.

The two storied house was built on the western side of the village approximately 100 yards from the pier, the ruins of which are still visible. The house was reputed to be named *Tigh Ban-tigheaona Larbhuir*, the House of the Lady of Lawers. The mysterious Lady of Lawers was reputed to be a Seer – a woman gifted with the power of wisdom and second sight. There are no written records left which confirm the true identity of the Lady of Lawers, however there is evidence to suggest that she was born in 1608 and that her name was Mary Campbell, originally a Stewart of Appin in Argyll and was brought to Loch Tay to marry John, the younger brother of Sir James Campbell, the 4th Laird of Lawers. The precedent for marriages between Campbells and females from the Stewart line having already been set in the 15th century by Sir Duncan Campbell, who had married Lady Marjorie Stewart, Sir Colin Campbell who had wed Mariot Stewart, the daughter of Sir Walter Stewart, and by 'Black' Duncan Campbell who had taken Elizabeth Stewart as his wife.

The Lady is believed to have arrived in Lawers between 1635 and 1645, with an escort of men called 'Na Chombaich', (The Companions). These men belonged to the Colquhoun Clan. Legend describes these men as the biggest and heaviest in Scotland. It was customary for such an escort to take up residence in their mistress's new home and remain as bodyguards. Kirk Session records from Kenmore refer to the Stewarts of Appin as having settled on Lochtayside at some time in the 17th century, bringing with them the Lady. Local tradition (according to *'In Famed Breadalbane'* written by the Rev. William Gillies of Kenmore in 1938) seems to assert that their arrival was in the form of an *'escort with the Lady'* and that the new family were known mysteriously as *Na Combaich* ('The Companions'). Perhaps this indicates the family's recognition of the Lady's importance and their desire to protect to her from the worst excesses of the Scottish Witch Hunts, so prevalent at the time (see later)?

Another theory suggests that the Lady of Lawers may have been the daughter of Sir James Campbell, the 4th Laird of Lawers, and that a male descendant of the Appin Stewarts came to Lawers in order to marry her. However, it seems unlikely that during the 17th century a male Stewart would have moved in order to accommodate the wishes of a woman, especially to the comparatively humble dwellings offered at Lawers.

1669 date stone from Lawers Church is still visible

The two-storey thatched house constructed for the Lady of Lawers and her husband actually belonged to Sir James Campbell, her husband's elder brother, meaning the Lady was only ever a tenant. Her family are, nonetheless, thought to be responsible for much of the construction of the old village. She also gave birth to a son, John Stewart, around 1645. However, it is possible her husband was one of the Lawers' Campbells killed at the Battle of Auldearn in May 1645, by the Duke of Montrose, meaning her son may have never met his father.

Lawers Church c1900

Many years later her son married and had a child of his own, (also named John Stewart) born in 1688.

The Lady of Lawers first prophecy is generally thought to have been made during the construction of the village church in 1669 by Sir James Campbell (the 6th Laird of Lawers), when she was approximately 60 years of age. It had been decided to build another church at Lawers because, since the destruction of the Chapel of Machuim twenty-four years earlier, Patrick Campbell, the Minister from Kenmore, had only been able to conduct open air services in good weather. When the building was nearing completion, the Lady of Lawers declared that the ridging stones, that were to clad the roof's apex, would never be placed there.

'Ma thèid a chlach mhullaich air Eaglais Labhuir cha bhi facal a labhair mise fior.'

(If the ridge stone goes atop of Lawers Church, no word I say will be true)

The ridging stones had already been brought ashore by boat from Kenmore and were laid out on the shoreline ready for use, so the builders and the villagers laughed off her prediction. However, that night a sudden and violent storm blew in and the stones were swept into the silt of Loch Tay. No attempt was ever made to recover them, and they were never placed on the church, thus cementing her reputation as a visionary. (It is said if a person knows where to look, the ridging stones can still be seen today). The ridge of the church was covered with another material instead. From that moment word of her uncanny predictions spread throughout the region. Locals and visitors alike began to pay attention to her ominous utterances and she was regarded with a new respect and even a certain fear. Many of her predictions did not come true until long after her death, perhaps meaning that the legend of her prophetic powers did not grow until after her lifetime.

Despite the pessimistic prediction, the church was completed in 1669, although perhaps not to the original specification. The building comprised a modest, single-storey harled affair, with broad eves and a jerkin-porch. At a later stage, a timber structure was added to the rear, signs of which were still visible as recently as 1971.

Once the church was completed, the Lady of Lawers planted an ash tree beside its north side and prophesied that, *'The tree will grow, and when it reaches the gable the church will be rent in twain* (split in two). *When it reaches the ridge, the House of Balloch will be without an heir'.* The Lady of Lawers also ominously added,

'Thigh sgiorradh obann air an duine a ghearras a chraoibh.'

(A sudden accident will befall the man who cuts the tree).

The tree finally grew to the height of the gable in 1843 and a thunderstorm destroyed the west loft of the church, collapsing the roof beams and rendering it derelict. 1843 was also the year in which the Church of Scotland split in the 'Disruption' when members of the congregation left to join the new Free

Church, which had been constructed in the new village of Lawers in 1833. Thus giving a literal and a metaphorical truth to the Lady's prediction.

The Rev. John Logan appears to have been the last Vicar at the old Lawers' Church, prior to the destruction of the building in 1843. He may well not have been present on that fateful day, however, as he had received an invitation to preside over the ordination of the Rev. Daniel Clarke at the free church in Aberfeldy.

In 1862, when the tree reached the roof ridge, John Campbell, 2nd Marquess of Breadalbane of the House of Balloch died with no heir, rendering the barony of Breadalbane extinct, thus bringing the next part of the prophecy true. Finally, on 30th June 1875 John Campbell, a farmer from the Milton of Lawers Farm, chopped the Lady's ash tree down, against the advice of his neighbours.

The ruins of Lawers Church

Shortly afterwards he was gored by his own Highland bull; and died from his injuries. His Death was officially recorded as *'Gangrene resulting from injury received by attack from bull.'*

Locals knew otherwise. As a result of John Campbell's terrible death and the fear it aroused, his farm assistant *'lost his reason, and had to be removed to the district asylum'*. Chillingly, to complete the curse,

Campbell's horse, which had been used to haul away the chopped down tree, inexplicably dropped dead.

Many years later, in 1950, Rev. Kenneth MacVicar of Kenmore Church was told by an old woman who was over ninety years of age at the time, that her mother had been in the boat which carried the dead John Campbell to his burial on the other side of the loch. When travelling across the loch it seemed certain to everyone in the boat that they would all be drowned as a fierce storm suddenly engulfed the boat. Somehow, they managed to reach Ardtalnaig on the other side, and placed the coffin on the shore. As they did so the loch mysteriously became calm and still. So strange was the incident that it made an impression on the woman for the remainder of her life.

Tales of the Lady's extraordinarily accurate prophesies were told all along the valley and a written record was kept in *'The Red Book of Balloch'*, a huge journal, stored in a container shaped like a barrel, secured by twelve iron clasps or rings, and kept in the Charter Room at Taymouth Castle. Unfortunately, the book vanished mysteriously at an unknown date. However, the prophecies were kept very much alive in the Gaelic oral tradition and were finally written down during the Victorian era, when interest in the Lady of Lawers was revived.

The Lady's prophesies often seemed to concern the Breadalbane heirs and their fortunes, for whom she held no great fondness. The two families had quarrelled during the time of Sir Duncan Campbell of Glenorchy, and the feud clearly remained. With reference to the lairds of Balloch (Taymouth) she said, *'John of the three Johns, the worst that has come, or will come; but nothing will be right until Duncan arrives.'* The third John in the Glenorchy line of chiefs was the first Earl who bears an unenviable reputation in history. Duncan was his eldest son, who might have been expected to succeed as second Earl of Breadalbane, but he was passed over by his father in favour of his brother John. The Lady of Lawers also forecast that *'the Campbells of Glenorchy would attain the height of their glory'* when a certain (unidentified) prominent rock would be covered by the trees growing around it. Unfortunately, the particular rock in question is not known; but it has been widely assumed to refer to the visit of Queen Victoria to Taymouth Castle in 1842, when the wealth and splendour displayed by the second Marquis had certainly never been equalled. Those living on Lochtayside at the time of Queen Victoria's visit scoured the skyline for the aforementioned rock, but on being unable to see one that matched the description, assumed the prophecy had come to pass.

During my research for the updated second edition of this book, I discovered two remarkable, and previously unmentioned, versions of prophecies spoken by the Lady of Lawers, which offer a slightly different version of the events surrounding the fate of her favourite ash tree and of her beloved village. Special credence can be added to these two newly discovered predictions, since they were recorded less than 140 years after her death; and by direct descendants of village residents, then subsequently reported in the *Dundee Courier* in 1863. The person responsible for preserving the exact wording of the Lady's utterances was himself an old man at the time of first hearing the prophecies, meaning little time had passed between first hearing the tales and transcribing them. This link with the past, unfortunately, remains a mystery; enigmatically referring to himself as 'One of Yourselves'.

According to this recently discovered source, the Lady 'predicted that, "even after the tree of the church should be cut down, that John of the four Johns would die, and a chief of the old race would succeed and restore the clan to their inheritance, and be the best superior that ever was in Breadalbane". *Strange to say, the tree was blown down by a storm some 18 months ago, and the Marquis' death happened in less than twelve months after'*.

'One of Yourselves' also reported that *'The Lady also* prophesied *"that John, the fourth of the line who disinherited his brother, would be the worst Superior of Breadalbane, and would be an evictor or clearance monger, and that people standing on a height near Lawers* [presumably atop Ben Lawers] *would only see three cottages where 20 were seen before." The late Marquis was the fourth John in prejudice of the true heir and an evictor. This literally came true not long ago.'* So certain was 'One of Yourselves' with the stories he had been told that he concluded his report by stating that; *'I believe there is not the smallest doubt as to the authenticity of these predictions; and the people about Lawers are able to say if the events referred to took place at the time and in the way predicted.'*

The Lady of Lawers foresaw the eventual break-up of the great Breadalbane Estates,

'Chaidh Braidalban cruinneachadh nan sguapan agus bidh e air a scap nam bideagan.'

(Breadalbane was gathered in sheathes and will be scattered in straws).

She also declared that *'the heirs of Breadalbane would have but one rent, and finally no rent at all.'*

The Breadalbane Estate was indeed originally amassed through the raiding and conquering of neighbouring lands. However, as the family fortune declined, due to extravagant expenditure, death duties and an inability to produce heirs, the estate was slowly sold off. And thus, two of the Lady's predictions came true simultaneously.

She also predicted many economic and social changes in the local area. Almost 200 years before the advent of the railways she spoke of *'fire-coaches'*, which would be seen crossing the Pass of Druimuachder (Drumochter), in the exact spot where the Highland Railway Line would eventually run. She spoke of *'ships driven by smoke on Loch Tay'*, 200 years before the Loch Tay Steamers arrived. It is extraordinary and undeniably eerie that, without any linguistic frame of reference, the Lady was able to accurately envision and describe steam engines and steam ships.

The Lady of Lawers foresaw there being *'a mill on every stream and a plough in every field.'* By the end of the eighteenth century, flax processing was a major industry in Perthshire with no less than twelve mills along the shores of Loch Tay alone (at Lawers, Fearnan, Killin, Remony, Finlarig, Morenish, Carwhin,

Crannich, Taymouth, Acharn, Ardeonaig and Cloichran), and nearly two hundred ploughs in use between Killin and Kenmore.

Many of her prophesies were pessimistic, but sadly accurate. *'The land will first be riddled then sifted of its people and the homes on Loch Tay shall become so scarce that a cock crowing will not be heard from one to the other, and the jaw of the sheep will drive the plough from the ground.'* Sadly, the Highland Clearances in the 1830's reduced the population of Loch Tayside from 3,500 to just a hundred or so, and the once heavily cultivated land was given over to flocks of Cheviot sheep.

Among the strangest of her prophecies predicted that the lands of the MacNab's at Killin would be added to the Breadalbane Estates when *'the branch of a fir tree fell and grafted to another tree.'* The MacNab lands were sold in 1828, and on the MacNab burial grounds on the island of Inchbuie, in the River Dochart, at Killin there is an enigmatic tree that perfectly matches the Lady's description. The fir tree did have a grafted branch, however – even more mysteriously – the grafted branch died when the MacNabs regained their ancestral estates in 1948.

Clan MacNab Burial Ground at Killin

'An old white horse will yet take the lineal heirs of the Breadalbane Campbells across Tyndrum Cairn and they will not return'. Not long after this ominous insight the thirty sons among the Breadalbane Campbells took part in a battle at Sron-a-chlachain, near Killin, and twenty-five were slain.

While forecasting the end of the church in Lawers she also predicted that if the cairn of stones built atop Ben Lawers (by sappers and miners) was to fall, the Disruption of the Church of Scotland would take place. Both these events occurred simultaneously in 1843.

Her predictions were, of course, spoken in Gaelic and handed down verbally from generation to generation, before eventually being transcribed and translated. With very few being able to read or write, the people of the Highlands possessed extraordinary powers of memory, together with a proud oral tradition of storytelling. Many could recite thousands of lines of poetry or folklore from memory. The introduction of writing, printing and books rather diminished this remarkable power and tradition. With uncanny accuracy the Lady of Lawers seems to have foretold this development *'Cuiridh ite geoidh an cuimhn' à duine.' (And the goose's feathers will drive their memories from men).* The quills of pens were traditionally made from the feathers of a goose. Perhaps the Lady of Lawer's special interest in this point was another example of her extraordinary insight? Did she foresee the building of schools and churches funded, built, and run by the Scottish Society for the Propagation of Christian Knowledge? These would result in many Highlanders learning to read and write in English. As time moved on there was less need for stories to be committed to memory and much of the once great Gaelic oral tradition was lost.

I also recently uncovered a 1909 newspaper article, which adds further detail to another of the Lady's prophecies,

'Curiously enough, a Loch Tayside proprietrix in the seventeenth century predicted that the "The sheep will put the plough out of the land, and then the deer will put the sheep off the land".'

A lengthy article followed, highlighting the problem of grazing sheep on rough pasture, and noting the eerie accuracy of the Lady's vision. Firstly, the sheep had, indeed, replaced the plough during the clearances and its immediate aftermath. Despite the sheep surviving well on the hillside pastures for the remainder of the 19th century, it was reported that by 1909 the land's ability to support sheep farming had reduced dramatically. One farmer reported that 'in 22 years, the sheep-carrying power of the land has declined from 1,000 sheep to 400 sheep.' A survey was carried out among the hill sheep farmers on north Lochtayside, with the majority concluding that the finer grasses were dying out, leaving only coarser grass and bracken, leading them to the conclusion that deer might provide the only profitable and sustainable income.

It seems that the Lady, speaking over 250 years before the event, had once again accurately predicted events along Lochtayside.

Her final prophecy again concerned the Breadalbanes and, once again, was less than complimentary, *'The last laird will pass over Glenogle with a grey pony leaving nothing behind.'* In 1948 the Countess of Breadalbane, the last of the family, who had been residing at Kinnell House at Killin, finally sold it and she crossed Glenogle on her way to the station at Killin in a trap drawn by a grey pony. The last laird of Breadalbane had departed leaving nothing behind.

Rather surprisingly, a remarkably similar story exists on the Isle of Jura. In fact, it may be that two separate folklore legends have merged together over time. During the early 1700s, it appears that the Campbell Laird of the island, along with evicting many of his tenants, had little time for seers and would forcibly remove them from his property whenever possible. He made the mistake of forcibly evicting one such soothsayer from the island, and in a parting shot she left him with this ominous prediction: *'The last Campbell Laird of Jura will be blind in one eye, and will leave the island with all of his belongings tied to a cart pulled by a lone white horse.'* This tale was well known among the inhabitants of Jura, and finally came to pass in 1938 when Charles Campbell, who had been blinded in the Great War, fell on hard times. As a consequence, he sold all his possessions and left the island with nothing but a horse and cart. In fact, even today, the Isle of Jura distillery produces a blend of whisky commemorating the story, called 'Prophecy'.

The Lady of Lawers died around the end of the 17th century. It was said that on the night she died a giant landslip occurred on the slopes of Ben Lawers and huge volumes of rock and earth cascaded in torrents into the Lawers Burn and into the loch – 'as though nature had been disturbed by her demise'. It is possible that the Lady of Lawers' death coincided with an earthquake, of which many have been recorded in the area; or that the true story of the great 1597 earthquake which struck the Highlands has become conflated with the legend that has grown around the Lady's death.

She is believed to be buried either at the entrance into the graveyard at Lawers, although no stone exists or, more probably, close to the ash tree that she planted in the churchyard. It was in this spot that her faithful servant, *'An Combach Ruadh'* (the red-haired companion), had also been buried, and it was her desire to rest near the man *'who had been her friend in the land of the Campbells'*. It is believed that her red-haired companion had accompanied her from Appin on her original journey to Lawers in the 1640s. The ghost of the forlorn lady is still reputed to haunt the ruins of the village. Indeed, those who venture during the hours of darkness into the remains of the village often claim to have sensed an unearthly presence.

Around the time of her death (and probably due to financial necessity) the Campbells of Lawers appear to have severed their connection with Loch Tayside, selling their lands to John Campbell the 1st Earl of Breadalbane. Their lands in and around Lawers were sold to the Breadalbane Estate and the family purchased an estate at Fordie in Strathearn. Overnight the inhabitants of Lawers became tenants of the Earls of Breadalbane. At this juncture the Breadalbane Campbells (of Glenorchy) already possessed enormous tracts of land, and through foul means and fair they continued to add to those estates. It was presumably this shift in power which had prompted many of the Lady's ominous prophecies concerning the Breadalbane family, and her antipathy towards them.

There seems to be little written evidence confirming the existence of the Lady of Lawers. Nevertheless, the legends surrounding her are so detailed, widespread and extensive that it cannot be doubted that she was a real, historical character. The Lady's ancestral lineage can be traced from her grandson John Stewart (born in 1688) to his son Angus Stewart (born 1715).

Angus in turn married Margaret McLachan, who bore him a son, Thomas Stewart, who was born in 1742 and died in 1806.

However, despite marrying Elizabeth Geddes in the 1760s, the couple did not produce any children, meaning there may not be any direct descendants of the Lady of Lawers. Whether her powers were handed down to any of her offspring is not known; or have been lost to the mists of time.

Even without the Campbells of Lawers the village continued to eke out an existence from the poor upland soils on Lochtayside. Cultivation was based on the runrig tenure system, under which fields were divided into strips and rotated to ensure every farmer had a share of the best land.

This antiquated arrangement gave the Highlanders a marginal existence. Tenancies seem to have been short lived. During the early part of the 17th century tenancies were initially granted for periods of between 3 and 5 years. However, by the latter part of the century, there appears to have been a high turnover of tenants, with very few families continuing at the same site for two generations. In 1670, it was recorded that only 9 of the 21 tenants were renewing the lease of their cottage and land.

The minister of Fortingall parish found it difficult to believe that they could exist on so little, and noted in the Kirk records, *'They bled their cows several times in the year, boiled the blood, eat a little of it like bread, and a most lasting meal it was.'* The Earls of Breadalbane attempted to relieve the pressure on the over-burdened and over-farmed land by building roads and bridges to open up the countryside and improve communications. They were instrumental in establishing flax processing as a major industry in Lawers, and all across Lochtayside, during the 18th century. Hugh Cameron, who was born at Lawers in 1705, constructed the lint mill and lime kiln at the eastern end of the village in 1761 and 1762 respectively. By 1770, the mill was producing 460 stone of flax per annum, requiring a new mill to be constructed in 1789 – for which builder's estimates still exist in the National Records of Scotland. These offer a fascinating insight into the construction and include accounts for digging foundations, quarrying stone, 4,300 slates, 440 slate nails, sheet-lead for the rigging, two doors, five windows and numerous other fittings.

The lime kiln has long gone, however the mill (which sat further up the hill close to the more modern bridge) has since been converted into a house. Hugh Cameron is said to have built almost a hundred mills in different parts of the country, and to have introduced spinning wheels into the Breadalbane estates. He died in 1817, at the extraordinary age of 112 years.

Houses built at Cuiltrannich for returning soldiers in 1797

A smithy, a meal mill and three smallholdings were constructed at Cuiltrannich, on 45 acres of land on the hillside along the burn, by Colonel Robertson of Lawers and his descendants. The land was leased to his widow Katherine Campbell in 1769 by the Breadalbane Estate at an annual rent of £305 (approximately £55,000 today!). Katherine's tenancy was renewed in 1771, before she assigned her lease to her son-in-law Duncan Campbell in 1778. The family built three smallholdings, plus a further two added later, probably constructed for soldiers from the Breadalbane 'Fencibles' Regiment who returned from duty in Europe in 1797.

We are lucky that John Farquarson's 1769 *Survey of the North Side of Loch Tay*, survives to provide us with some detail of the old village. The Earl of Breadalbane had commissioned Farquarson to provide him with a detailed account of his land and holdings. One can imagine that many of the tenants may have been less than willing to provide Farquarson with full details of their assets – fearing a possible rent rise – however, the record seems to be a substantial one.

Farquarson describes the farming land around Lawers as follows, *'The infields are extremely good and deep soil, the outfields by the lochside are thin steep and sandy.'* The Survey also predates the earliest official census and provides us with a unique record of those living in and around Lawers in 1769.

One wonders if any descendants of these families still live in the surrounding areas, and whether the spelling of their surnames has changed over the centuries?

CROFTANTAYAN (3 ploughs) – Possessors (tenants) are: Joseph Man, Pat McAllantich, Hugh Dore, Duncan McAnucater, Colonel Campbell, and Duncan McNaughtown. The farm is leased to the six tenants for 21 years, with the rent fixed at £48 15s 6d, and twenty bolls of oatmeal. Each tenant to furnish Lord Breadalbane with a man and a horse for ten days. Their stocking of the farm is restricted to 65 cows, 30 horses and 230 sheep.

TOMB AND KIEN CROFT (2 ploughs) – Possessors are: Robert Man, Joseph McInucator, John McDugal and Donald Mcay. Fine infields. Plenty of limerock. Rent £22 11s and 8 bolls of oatmeal.

MILTOWN OF LAWERS – The most delightful place on the lochside having a fine view of Ardtalnaig on the south side. Possessed by Colonel Campbell's widow. The family also keep an Under-Miller for the Meal Mill.

Farquarson points out that the buildings at Tomb and Milton of Lawers seem to have been of a superior quality than those of the remaining thirteen tenants in Lawers, being stone built with secure roofing. The study also indicates that every tenant was required to provide manpower and horses *'immediately when required'* to *'lead peat from the hills and for two days a harvest.'*

New arrivals bolstered the population of the village, including Hugh McDougall. Following his marriage to Mary Ferguson in Fearnan, his family moved west along the loch to Lawers and leased a cottage at Cuiltrannich.

Farmers' sons were even sent to England to study new methods of agriculture. On the hillsides above Lawers, the process of replacing the old runrig system began. New, compact farms were laid out; the rotation of crops was introduced and winter feeds were improved. By the end of the 18th century the Minister of Killin noted that their *'wise plans'* had ushered in a period of stability and relative prosperity so that the people of Lawers *'in general, were in easy rather than in affluent circumstances.'*

Herman Moll's map of Loch Tay, 1732

The Ministers of Kenmore appear, as a rule, to have personally conducted the services at Lawers. However, in 1714, the Rev. Alexander Comrie, then Parish Minister, installed the Rev. Robert Stewart as the Vicar at Lawers, with the power to hold sessions, baptise and marry. He was instructed (according to the Kenmore Kirk Session Records) to *'keep a register of all he did, and send a scroll to Kenmore, so as not to wrong the clerk, the beadle, and the box'.* The Rev. Stewart was twice married, and died in 1729, leaving by his first wife four sons, James, laird of Killiechassie, Duncan, laird of Blackhall, Alexander, laird of Cloichfoldich, and Robert, Laird of Derculich. During the time he was at Lawers, *'he neither kept register or scrolls, and monopolised for himself all the dues payable to the Clerk, Bedal, and Box'*, according to Scottish Ecclesiastical records, which may help account for the poor physical health of the building.

Little, by way of records, survive from the original church in Lawers, however an entry was compiled during the 1830s and 1840s for *The New Statistical Account of Scotland* which does provide a little information on the Rev. Colin McVean, who became Minister at Lawers Church in 1791, before taking up the vacant living at Kenmore Church in 1794:

'There is a chapel at Lawers, on the north side of Loch Tay, where the ministers of Kenmore and Weem preach occasionally. Here the Society for Propagating Christian Knowledge established, in the year 1790, a mission, on a fund mortified by the late Lady Glenorchy (Breadalbane), *of which they have management. Out of this fund one half of the missionary's salary is paid; the bearers pay the other. Lord Breadalbane gives a*

manse and glebe. In this mission the present minister of Kenmore officiated, for about three years previous to his settlement there, which was on the 13th March 1794.'

Ironically, by the time this account was published in 1845 the church had already been destroyed and the entire congregation migrated to the new Free Church, built in 1833. A 16-inch uninscribed bell, thought to date to the early 1700s, was hung in the new church, and was probably moved from the old church at the time of the disruption.

By the middle of the 18th century the north side of Loch Tay was provided with three public schools. One was situated at Tomachrocher in Morenish, one in Lawers (at the top of the Pier Road), and the third at Boreland in Fearnan. From a report on the state of religion in the Highlands, made at the instigation of the General Assembly in 1760, it was noted that the *'number of scholars attending Lawers school during the wintertime was between fifty and sixty, while at Killin there were only thirty-four'*. The teacher at Lawers school, in addition to a small sum paid from the Royal Bounty, received from the Earl of Breadalbane a salary of a hundred merks a year, and was also provided with a free house, garden, and fuel.

In 1774 an incident occurred which was recorded, thus giving us a valuable insight into the mood of the community. Donald McVean had taken a lease on the mill croft in 1732 and had spent considerable amounts of his own money on improving it. When a new miller was appointed for Lawers the villagers wished to house him in the croft occupied by Donald

McVean. It emerged that McVean's lease had actually expired some four years earlier. Without a croft it was feared the new miller would resign. The community petitioned the property's owner Duncan Campbell, son-in-law of Catherine Campbell, who promptly repossessed the croft, fixed a new rent, and forced the other tenants in the village to erect a stone dyke to divide the croft from his home. It appears that the Campbells were not to be argued with! No record existed of what became of Donald McVean, who must have been an old man by this point.

Lawers, and the areas to the east and west, seems to have reached a peak of population and activity between 1710 and 1840. From that point onwards a general decline appears to have taken place. The Minister of Kenmore recorded a population increase of 12% in the 45 years between the Webster's census returns of 1755 and 1800. Smallpox inoculations certainly helped to reduce the death rate from the disease. And, as potatoes grew to become the staple diet, people's general health and, consequently, their survival rates improved. This was offset by the gradual depopulation of people from the more remote hillside areas who were no longer needed to farm the land, due to the increase in sheep farming (as predicted by the Lady of Lawers). The Minister of Kenmore also made note of the extra profitability for the Breadalbane Estate, generated from the land by the removal of smallholding tenants, in favour of larger farmsteads. Forced off their farms during these clearances, the landless refugees migrated to the towns and found employment in service, as workers in the flax industry or as masons, joiners, shoemakers, blacksmiths, farriers, and other crafts.

Many emigrated to America, Australia, Canada and New Zealand.

Lawers suffered a tragic loss in March 1821 when Duncan Campbell, who had recently joined the Perthshire Militia as a Lieutenant, had been stood fishing on a rock in a middle of Lawers' burn when a sudden torrent of water rushing down the hill swept him off the rock and into the loch. His body was carried out a considerable distance into the water and, despite efforts to rescue him, he tragically drowned.

The Mill at Lawers (now converted to holiday accommodation)

Whilst the houses in Lawers managed to escape the worst of the Clearances, developments in 1834 sped up the process of depopulation. The Second Marquis allowed his factor, James Wyllie, to evict families on Lochtayside and to populate his farms with Cheviot sheep. The evictions were carried out with ruthless severity. No sooner were the tenants turned out of their homes than the thatch was set on fire to prevent them from returning. One villager, who had assisted James Wyllie with the evictions, was himself evicted, and forced to emigrate. As he was leaving the township someone asked him, *'Is there no more dirty work to be done in Breadalbane so they are sending you away?'*

Lady of Lawers House c1900

Between 1834 and 1838, fourteen families had been removed forcibly from Rhynachuilig, twelve from Edramchie, thirteen from Kiltyrie, nine from Cloichran, and nineteen from the farm of Acharn. Although there is no mention of Lawers in this dismal roll call it seemed to have a draining effect on the remaining tenants in the village. Work opportunities outside the community were diminished and those remaining in Lawers feared for their livelihood. The tenants of Lawers rented their properties from the Breadalbane Estate but were afforded little in the way of tenants' rights. Few of the residents had any security of tenure and there was no assurance that they would be compensated by the Breadalbane Estate for any improvements that they made to their properties.

Ruins of Lawers Church (photographed in the 1970s)

In 1840 the then Minister of Kenmore observed that *'the buildings, in general, are in an indifferent state'*. By the time of the 1841 Census just 17 people were recorded as living in Lawers, all crammed into just a few houses. Rents had tripled in the previous 50 years, meaning that basic economic necessity forced families to either share accommodation meant for far fewer people, or simply seek their fortune elsewhere.

The regular ferries that ran across the loch between Lawers and Ardeonaig, and also between Fearnan and Acharn, ceased to operate at this time too. The Clearances effectively meant there were no longer enough customers left to support a ferryman.

Despite the roof of the church collapsing in 1843, it appears that the Rev. Stewart from Killin visited Lawers occasionally to deliver sermons to the remaining residents. Whether these sermons took place in the ruins of the old church (in the days before health and safety!) or by the loch side is not known. A newspaper article from 1863 does state, however, that the remains of the church were used as a byre (shed) for the few remaining cattle. A sad and ignominious final chapter for the building.

Breadalbane Fencibles Regiment pendant

A dramatic incident occurred in Lawers in 1850 when, what was reputed to be, the world's largest Scots fir tree was blown down in a severe storm. When the gigantic tree lay felled on the ground, the villagers measured its circumference at a point one foot from its base. The mighty fir boasted a girth of 17 feet 7 inches!

By the midpoint of the 19th century only one hundred inhabitants were recorded as living on the whole of Lochtayside.

When the Second Marquis tried to raise a Regiment, as his father had successfully done in the 18th century, he could find no recruits. An old man in Lawers is reputed to have growled at him to *'Put your red coats on the backs of the sheep that have replaced the men!'*

Steadily the remaining population dwindled. The younger residents moved away; and the elder inhabitants gradually passed away. The *'Queen of Beauty'* horsedrawn coaches began their daily journeys from Birnam to Callander, along what is now the A827, which was fast becoming a more convenient travel route than by boat along the loch. As postal services became established with the introduction of the 'uniform postal rate', the adhesive stamp in 1837, and the 'Penny Black' one year later, these helped to increase the importance of the road as the main artery, progressively diminishing the viability of the old village and its loch side location. In addition, the building of the Ben Lawers Hotel and Inn helped establish what would become the current village of Lawers, further reducing the relevance of the original community.

As time marched on, the few remaining tenants gradually reduced in number. In 1874 Catherine Stewart, daughter of Archibald Stewart, one of the last remaining young ladies in Lawers, married and moved away to Edinburgh. John Campbell, the occupier of the Milton of Lawers farm, passed away in 1875. Six years later John MacNaughton, one of the few remaining tenants in the community, died at the age of 81.

Lawers was also affected by one of the perennial crimes suffered by farmers in Perthshire. In one of many such incidents Peter MacMartin, a local sheep farmer, accused Donald McDougall, from Tomrara in Lawers, of sheep stealing. In 1877 this was considered a grave offence resulting in a court appearance for McDougall and, no doubt, created a great deal of local tension. Shortly afterwards, Donald McDougall relocated to Edinburgh and became a liquor merchant. The following year Donald MacMartin of Easter Cloan at Lawers suffered the loss of 37 sheep, which were stolen by Peter Campbell of Balnearn, who fraudulently forged a bill of sale for the purchase of the flock. The serious nature of the crime is highlighted by the 12-month prison sentence Peter Campbell received.

Lawers' sheep were considered to be hardy and valuable stock and regularly featured at the Aberfeldy and Stirling Auction Marts well into the 20th century. Again, in 1895, Peter MacMartin, and another Lawers' sheep farmer Duncan Anderson, accused John Cameron of 'sheep-worrying' and sued him via the Perth Sheriff's Court, claiming that Cameron's dog had caused significant damage to their stock. After a hotly contested case, damages of £15 (approximately £2,000 today) were awarded to Messrs MacMartin and Anderson.

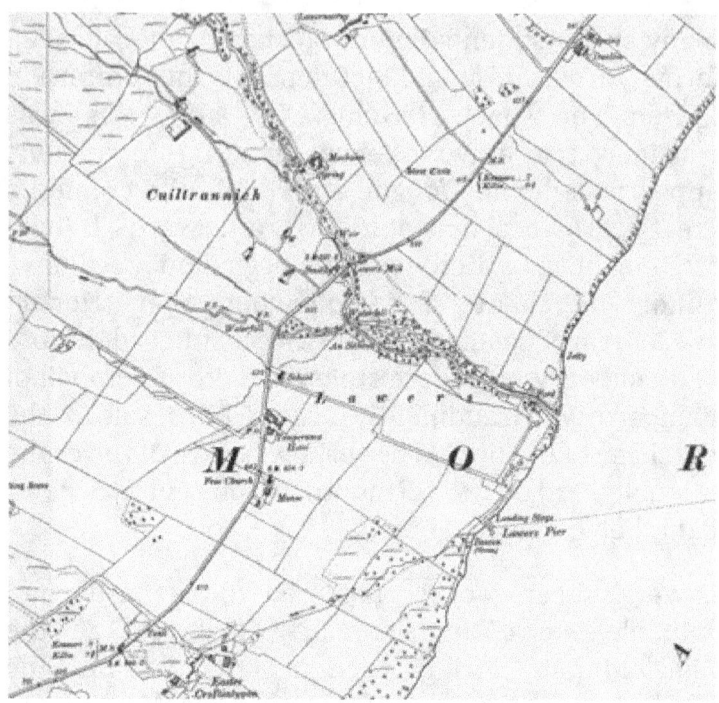

1882 Map showing Lawers

William Marshall, whilst travelling in Perthshire in 1879, and compiling his book *Historic Scenes in Perthshire*, added some extra detail to the story of the Lady of Lawers. Marshall noted the derelict condition of the church and, on speaking to the few remaining villagers, was informed that the Lady of Lawers was buried near the ash tree she had planted in the churchyard.

In a slightly different version of the legend (mentioned earlier) Marshall was told that, before dying, she had prophesied that:

'a tree would grow out of her grave in the churchyard of Lawers, and that when it should be as high as the gable of the old church, such evil times would over-take the house of Breadalbane as would threaten its extinction, and that the greatest and most perplexing doubts would arise as to its rightful heir.'

At the time of William Marshall's book this prophecy had recently seemed to have reached its conclusion. The 2nd Marquess of Breadalbane had passed away in 1862, without leaving a direct heir. A five-year court battle then ensued, eventually culminating with Gavin Campbell inheriting the estate.

By 1891 the population of Lawers had reduced to just seven, and the school numbers had diminished further. The last remaining seven inhabitants of the village all occupied the Pier Master's House. Although the Clearances had finished, the leaching of the rural population into the towns and cities continued. The new Free Church in Lawers also closed. The advent of electricity, gas, telephone, and other modern comforts in the larger towns changed the landscape forever; and with it, the attraction of the remote Highland life. Duncan Campbell was one such resident. Formerly the miller in the village, and a popular local figure, he moved away to become a farmer during the 1880s. He died in suspicious circumstances in 1904, at the age of 60, when his lifeless body was discovered, with a six-inch gash on the side of his head, lying by the side of the Weem to Strathtay road. In the absence of any other evidence, his death was assumed to be a tragic accident.

The sheep farmer Duncan Anderson (mentioned above) had a son named Hector who became yet another Lawers' resident to move away from Lochtayside – although in happier circumstances. Hector Anderson, reputed to be the cleverest person to ever have been born in Lawers, attended Strathallan School and George Watson's College where he finished top of his class. In 1900, at the age of 21, he was awarded a £60 scholarship from the Edinburgh Perthshire Association to enable him to study at Oriel College, Oxford. Hector would receive an exhibition from his college for his outstanding achievement in the classics, qualifying with honours. After studying for an M.A. in Edinburgh he became His Majesty's Inspector of Training Colleges in the Cape Colonies.

Rev. Hugh MacMillan published *The Highland Tay* in 1901, in which he eloquently described his journeys around Loch Tay. He was particularly taken with the old village of Lawers:

'The burying-ground of the locality, called Cladh Machuim, lies a short distance to the eastward, across the burn of Lawers; and the original church must have stood on that site in pre-Reformation times. In this charming, secluded spot, with the waters of the Loch laving the pebbly beach below, and the lofty peak of Ben Lawers looking proudly down upon it, are interred Mcdiarmids, Macgregors, Macmartins, Camerons, Andersons, Crerars, and Campbells, whose ancestors long ago were at perpetual feud with one another, but now all rest under the common sod.'

By 1909 the Ben Lawers Hotel would provide telegraph and postal services, as well as offering residents fishing rights on the loch, effectively removing another source of income from the old village.

Without any hope of generating a sustainable living from the old mill, Duncan McLellan appealed to the Perth County Valuation Appeals Court in September 1915. He claimed that the Mill of Lawers was no longer a working mill, therefore he could no longer afford to pay Lord Breadalbane the previously agreed rent of £5 12s 6d. Lord Breadalbane's solicitor, Mr Boyd, argued that as Duncan McLellan was still technically the tenant, the full amount should be paid. Duncan McLellan admitted to still using the old mill building as a storeroom. He lost the case and the rent remained at £5. Not surprisingly, without any income, the mill was soon vacated and left to crumble, along with the remainder of the village.

The Macnab family of Drumglass Farm, just to the east of the graveyard at Lawers, received tragic news at Christmas 1915. The family's youngest son James, aged only 24, died in Alexandria, of wounds received while serving with the 3rd Scottish Horse Brigade in the Dardanelles.

One of the final burials to take place in Lawers – while the village was still occupied – took place in 1921. William McPherson, son of John and Jessie McPherson from Acharn, served as a Private in the 4th Battalion, Seaforth Highlanders during the Great War. William was born on 13th April 1882 and had previously taken up his father's trade of shoemaker, before enlisting. Despite surviving the war, he sadly died of related injuries suffered (Pulmonary Tuberculosis, which was contracted by many serving soldiers). William was buried at Lawers cemetery on 22nd May 1921 – the same day that the Great War memorial was unveiled in nearby Kenmore. Sadly, as the War memorial had already been carved, the name of William McPherson appears to have 'slipped through the net' and has never been added to the 32 Lochtayside names remembered there.

William McPherson

Tragically, William's younger brother Duncan was also killed in action on the 11th April 1917, at the age of 25, during the Battle of Vimy Ridge, and buried in Givenchy Road Canadian Cemetery. Duncan had been working in Canada at the time of enlistment.

The burial of William McPherson at Lawers has given the graveyard official designation as a Commonwealth War Grave, meaning it remains the best-preserved part of the old village of Lawers. Today, visitors to this charming and tranquil place, may be grateful as without this official designation the graveyard would have almost certainly fallen into as bad a state of disrepair as the remainder of the village. A correspondent, writing for the Dundee Advertiser in July 1889, recorded that,

'To-day I visited this little burying-ground but was disappointed to find it in a most discreditable condition. The walls are in a tumble-down state, and the graves are quite overgrown with a tangled maze of

long grass and rank weeds, so much so, that only the tops of the larger gravestones are visible.'

SS Lady of the Lake at Lawers Pier c.1890

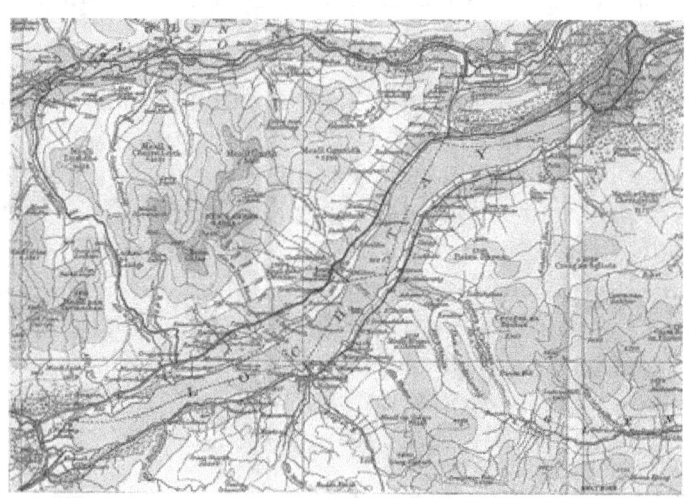

c.1900 map showing ferry routes

> ## LOCH TAY
> ## STEAMBOAT SERVICE.
>
> THE Public are respectfully informed that the STEAMBOAT SERVICES for PASSENGER and GOODS TRAFFIC on LOCH TAY will be RESUMED on MONDAY, 20th February, 1922, on and from which date the Service will be as follows:—
>
> | | a.m. | | Noon. |
> |---|---|---|---|
> | Kenmore Pier lve. | 9.30 | Glasgow (Buchanan Street), ... lve. | 12.0 |
> | Fearnan .... ,, | 9.53 | | a.m. |
> | Ardtalnaig .... ,, | 10.13 | Edinburgh (Princes | |
> | Lawers .... ,, | 10.35 | Street), ... lve. | 11.50 |
> | Ardeonaig .... ,, | 11.5 | Oban, ... lve. | 11.45 |
> | Killin Pier arr. | 12.0 | | |
>
> | | p.m. | | p.m. |
> |---|---|---|---|
> | Oban .... arr. | 4.45 | Killin Pier .. lve. | 3.30 |
> | Edinburgh (Princes | | Ardeonaig .... ,, | 4.10 |
> | Street) .... arr. | 4.43 | Lawers ...... ,, | 4.35 |
> | Glasgow (Buchanan | | Ardtalnaig .. ,, | 4.55 |
> | Street) .... arr. | 4.20 | Fearnan ...... ,, | 5.20 |
> | | | Kenmore Pier arr. | 6.0 |
>
> Freight Traffic of all descriptions will be accepted for transit by Steamer or Barge, and all information as to Rates can be ascertained on application to the Pier Masters at the different Piers, or to the Steamboat Office, Kenmore.
>
> BY ORDER.

Loch Tay Steamers Timetable

There seemed to be some hope for the beleaguered village of Lawers when the newly launched Loch Tay steamship the *S.S. Lady of the Lake* began calling in 1882, as part of the new Loch Tay excursions designed for well off Victorian visitors.

The pier at Lawers was extended and improved, to offer a safe mooring for the 70ft *S.S. Lady of the Lake*, with her 60ft keel.

However, it does not appear to have provided a boost for the community. The decaying, empty homesteads providing little more than a temporary distraction for the disembarking visitors as they walked the mile up the track, either to begin their ascent of Ben Lawers, or stroll to the Ben Lawers Hotel for some light refreshment, before continuing their onward journey to Killin.

Lord Breadalbane put forward a motion to the Perth Roads Committee in 1895 for an improvement to the Lawers Pier Road, stating that the Loch Tay Steamers could be used for the transportation of goods thus saving several miles of arduous road travel; if the road surface could be improved. Such had the importance of the old village slipped in the memories of the Committee; that many did not even realise the road still existed. Despite the committee's apparent indifference to the condition of the road surface, Perth County Council did agree to some improvements being carried out in early 1896. Mr Bell, the County Road Surveyor, organised the clearing and gravelling of the track, which was carried out in the spring.

Although this improved the short climb from the loch to the main road, it does not seem to have brought any long-term economic benefit for the few remaining residents of Lawers.

Unfortunately, the Loch Tay Steamboat Service always struggled financially; and services became less frequent. After a gap in services during the Great War the business ceased trading in the 1920s. Following the collapse of the company the last remaining family finally abandoned the Pier Master's House in 1926; and moved from the lochside settlement, leaving the village empty and the dry-stone wall and thatched roofed cottages to decay slowly into their present state. The break-up of the great Breadalbane estates in the 1920s also removed the final link with the land tenure system of the past.

Lawers School

Miss Margaret Macfarquhar was appointed Headmistress at Lawers School in 1924, but with no children remaining in the old settlement of Lawers, numbers were small and the school's days were numbered.

Now the encroaching trees and undergrowth are gradually cloaking what remains of a community that had existed for almost a thousand years. Together with the ravages of the Highland weather there may soon be little left to remind us of a once unique way of life. Only the perfectly tended graveyard (with its designation as an official Commonwealth War Grave) stands defiant to the march of the centuries; offering the visitor the chance to step back in time, for the briefest of moments.

The abandoned settlement of Lawers does live on, however, in the legend of the mysterious Lady of Lawers. Her chilling prophecies are still discussed by those born and bred in the area. Several intriguing questions still remain unanswered.

Firstly, why is there no record of any predictions by the Lady of Lawers prior to 1669, when she had already reached the comparatively old age of 60? Conceivably she did not make any, or perhaps they were merely ignored? It could be that she did claim to have the powers of second sight as a younger woman. However, because her visions did not immediately come to pass, they have been simply forgotten or not handed down from generation to generation.

One highly probable theory is that the Lady of Lawers wisely kept quiet about her gift of prophecy. Born in 1608, she grew up during the height of the Scottish witch hunts and persecutions. The passing of the Witchcraft Act in 1563 made witchcraft, or even consulting with witches, capital crimes. King James VI of Scotland then increased the public fear of witchcraft by publishing his defence of witch-hunting in his book entitled *Daemonologie* in 1597. An estimated 4,000 people in Scotland were tried for witchcraft in a one-hundred-year period from 1563 – almost twice the rate achieved in neighbouring England. During the lifetime of the Lady of Lawers there were major series of witchcraft trials in 1628–31, 1649–

50 and 1661–62, as well as bitter memories of the great persecutions of 1597. 75% of all those accused were women. Modern estimates indicate that more than 1,500 persons were executed; most were strangled and then burned. The witch hunts subsided

during English occupation under Oliver Cromwell in the 1650s, and the Privy Council of Scotland passed legislation to limit arrests, prosecutions, and torture in the 1660s. This coincided with a generally growing scepticism in the later part of the 17th century. Perhaps the Lady of Lawers, and other residents of the community, merely felt able to openly disclose predictions and insights that they previously could not, for fear of persecution?

Further evidence to support this theory was uncovered by the University of Glasgow in recent research. While details of numerous witch hunts were uncovered in Appin during the 17th century, including that of Donald McIlmichall, tried in Inveraray in 1677, none seem to have occurred in the area around Lochtayside. The Celtic legends of Appin are crammed with stories of soothsayers, magic and prophets. Was the Lady of Lawers perhaps descended from a long line of seers and inherited her powers (in the Celtic tradition)? Perhaps the Stewarts of Appin were keen to move their mysterious seeress to an area of comparative safety, and a marriage among the Campbells of Lawers provided the perfect opportunity? The theory is an interesting one. It is, after all, certainly coincidental that the Lady's first recorded prophecy occurred shortly after the legislation to limit the persecution of witches was enacted, and only while she resided in Lawers.

Further evidence to support the notion that the Lady felt able to speak freely by 1669, can also be garnered from two highly influential books which were published at the time.

Firstly, in 1658, before we are aware of any public prophecy by the Lady of Lawers, the following publication highlighted the dangers to the public of anyone displaying any unusual behaviour or gift, "*A Treatise of Specters, or AN HISTORY of Apparitions, Oracles, Prophecies, and Predictions, With Dreams, Visions and Revelation*"

With highly inflammatory language as highlighted below, it is, perhaps, little wonder that the Lady remained reticent for a number of years:

"*The Predictions of Soothsayers, and lewd Priests. The cosening tricks and superstitious observations of senseless Augurers and Soothsayers (contrary to Philosophy, and without authority of Scripture), are very ungodly and ridiculous.*"

'Cosening' is an archaic word meaning the art of acting deceitfully.

The text goes on to describe the contrast between the prophecies of God as the "*one faith always true*", against the words of the soothsayer which are described as "*horrible lyes and cosenages*", "*the work of counterfeits and coseners*", and as "always proceeding from the devil, and are always false". *The book also asks the question, to its nervous and God-fearing readership* "What bargain hath the soothsayer made with the devil? How chanceth that we hear not of this bargain in the Scriptures?"

However, with the advent of a more enlightened era, heralded by the reinstatement of King Charles II to the throne in 1660, more progressive and liberal thinkers countered these arguments. A highly influential series of manuscripts collated by Reginald Scot, first printed in France the 1650s and eventually published in 12 huge volumes in Britain in 1665, entitled:

"The Discovery of Witchcraft: Proving That the Compacts and Contracts of Witches With Devils and all Infernal Spirits or Familiars, are but Erroneous Novelties and Imaginary Conceptions"

John Campbell, the 1st Earl of Loudoun, also felt able to write to local witch trial committees advising them that they could not rely on the first confession of a witch, obtained under duress by an appointee of the church, but should rely on further confessions obtained in a different manner. Perhaps by 1669 the Lady now felt safe to openly report her visions; and perhaps she was even able to persuade John Campbell to act as he did? Her prolific utterances in the years following 1669

until her death, seem to certainly imply an era in which she felt more comfortable to speak more freely.

A further conundrum, which has perplexed many, and seems at odds with the unnerving accuracy of the Lady of Lawers' many other predictions, are the three prophecies that have not yet come to pass – or have they?

'When the Boar's Stone at Fearnan is toppled, a strange heir will come to Balloch.'

'A ship driven by smoke will sink in Loch Tay with great loss of life.'

'The time will come when Ben Lawers will become so cold that it will chill and waste the land for seven miles.'

However, it may be possible, with a little imagination and research, to explain events in such a way that might suggest a degree of truth and accuracy in these predictions too.

'When the Boar's Stone at Fearnan is toppled, a strange heir will come to Balloch (Taymouth).'

The Boar's Stone *(Clach an Tuirc)* is an ancient cup-marked rock of immense size. Its weight has been estimated at 200 tonnes.

During the Lady of Lawer's lifetime the Bronze Age rock lay in a field at Fearnan. *Clach an Tuirc* is a mighty boulder, and it is difficult to conceive of it ever tumbling over; however, the Lady's prophecy could be said to have at least partly come true, since the rock has clearly toppled and now forms part of the garden wall of a cottage on the Fearnan to Fortingall Road. How and when it fell, and how it was moved is not known. It could also be argued that since the last Earl of Breadalbane passed away, the Taymouth Castle Estate has seen a succession of unusual 'heirs', all taking up residence, only for their tenure to ultimately fail. Ranging from a Hydro Hotel, to the Ministry of Defence, the Polish Army and, more recently, various leisure investment consortiums, each new 'heir' to the Taymouth Castle Estate has failed to secure a long-term future for the once proud Breadalbane Estate.

'A ship driven by smoke will sink in Loch Tay with great loss of life.'

During the Lady's lifetime a drowning accident occurred on Loch Tay, in which a number of people lost their lives. Lochtayside was deeply affected, however the Lady of Lawers predicted even further loss of life. *'A ship driven by smoke will sink in Loch Tay with great loss of life.'* Whilst the sinking element of her prophecy does not appear to have (yet!) come true, the Lady of Lawers successfully predicted the appearance of steamships on the Loch 200 years before their arrival. The prophecy certainly helped to contribute to the ultimate demise of the Loch Tay Steamers. Many Victorians and Edwardians refused to venture on the ships because of the fear caused by her forecast. Those brave souls that did undertake their Loch Tay excursion, aboard the Lady of the Lake on 7th June 1913 may have thought the Lady's prediction was about to come true.

A ferocious storm battered the loch, the worst in living memory, and the vessel was pitched furiously from side to side. Huge waves, the likes of which had never been seen, lashed the decks and the passengers were forced to huddle in the saloon as the water smashed against the windows. Luckily no one was seriously hurt, although many of the passengers were badly shaken.

The Lady's prophecy offered no recognisable time limit; therefore, it may yet still come to pass. Let us hope that is one prediction that does not materialise. Perhaps the name 'Loch Tay' has itself become 'cursed'? During the research for this book, I have discovered no less than three ships bearing the name 'Loch Tay' have sunk! The *SS Loch Tay* was grounded and sunk in Gibraltar in the 1920s. The *Loch Tay FV* (Fishing Vessel LT1103) was sunk by German U-Boat UB-18, captained by Otto Steinbrinck, on 17th July 1916, in seas ten miles NNE of the Haisborough Lightvessel. And in Jamaica a dredging ship, also called *Loch Tay,* sank after colliding with a harbour wall in 1928.

'The time will come when Ben Lawers will become so cold that it will chill and waste the land for seven miles.'

This final prophecy is somewhat difficult to interpret; and has therefore been generally assumed to have not yet been fulfilled.

However, it might be less literal; merely referring to the clearances, or the poor fertility of the land for farming. That is not to say that it could not be taken literally. There have been many bad winters in Highland Perthshire since the 1700s, in which temperatures have plummeted, the ground has frozen, and cultivating the land has been rendered impossible. Such winters occurred in 1811, 1904, 1913, 1946 and 1949. In the winter of 1963 the temperatures in Perthshire did not rise above zero degrees centigrade for 48 consecutive days and roads between Kenmore and Killin were impassable for weeks.

The surrounding fields froze like iron and farmers struggled to care for their animals. As recently as 2010 and 2011 the cold weather froze the farmland surrounding Ben Lawers into a rock-hard state.

The road crossing from the village of Lawers to Glenlyon is frequently impassable in winter, due to ice and snow.

Perhaps, most tantalisingly of all, a report from 1913 that seems to mirror the exact wording of the Lady's prophecy. In January of that year a snowstorm of such severity ravaged Ben Lawers that eight inches of snow fell on the fields, creating drifts of seven feet in depth.

'All the hill roads were blocked and the fields covered. The Post Office mail driver (then known as the 'motormail') *became stuck at Lawers and could not return to Aberfeldy due to heavy snow.'* The *Dundee Courier* reported. *'Even a horse could not cross the fields and the postman became stranded. In the face of a blinding snowstorm and over four feet of snow on the road, the land surrounded Ben Lawers was laid waste for a distance of seven miles. Mr James Campbell, shouldered his mail bag and tramped the distance from Lawers to Fearnan.'*

There are two further stories about the Lady of Lawers that are unanswered, but relate to lost or missing clues, rather than predictions.

Firstly, she inscribed the following quotation on a peculiarly shaped stone and placed it near the summit of Ben Lawers:

'Caith mar a gheibh, is gheibh mar- a chaitheas, Caomhain 's co dha? Cuimhnich am bas.'

Translated into English the wording on the stone read as follows:

'Spend as you get, and get as you spend, Save, and for whom? Remember death.'

Despite sitting undisturbed on the summit of Ben Lawers for almost 200 years – and its existence being well-known to locals – the stone disappeared sometime towards the end of the 19th century, having probably been carried away by an antique collector. Whether any misfortune befell them is unknown!

The second mystery relates to the location of the Lady of Lawers' well. According to *Survivals In Beliefs Among The Celts*, written by George Henderson in 1911, the Lady was remembered in the name of a healing spring:

"As is well known, Beltane, or the first day of May, was one of the sacred days of the ancient Highlanders. In my grandfather's youth it was the custom for the young men and maidens of Lawers to climb to the summit of Ben Lawers on that day to see the sun rise, and it was a race between the young men to see which of them would first reach and drink out of a tobar (spring) *called 'Fuaran Bhain-tighearna Labhair' the Lady of Lawers's Well, which in former times was supposed to possess great curative virtues, especially for children, and its fame had spread far and wide. Sick children were brought from Rannoch and other distant places to be bathed in, or sprinkled with, its water. The sick child was placed between two stones on the brink of the tobar on Beltane eve, and his parents watched through the night by his side. When the sun was visible the child was dipped in the pool, or sprinkled with the water, accordingly, as his strength allowed. The parents, on*

leaving the tobar were mindful to put a coin or some offering in it. Many years ago a shepherd found an old Scots coin in or at the tobar, and it was in his possession for a long time."

The location of this well is unknown and remains another tantalising secret in the search to unravel the mystery of the Lady of Lawers.

Although the Lady of Lawers died more than 300 years ago, fascination in her true identity and the accuracy of her prophecies is still talked about along the shores of Lochtayside. Occasionally interest is re-awakened. During the break-up of the Breadalbane Estate in the 1920s the Perthshire Advertiser commented on the similarity between the predictions of the Lady of Lawers and the demise of the Breadalbane line.

Small scale archaeological excavations took place in the 1930s to the northwest of the church, which uncovered part of a boundary wall, a cobbled trackway, and a James III farthing coin from the 1480s.

In 1938 when the Rev. Gillies' book *In Famed Breadalbane* was published it sparked a series of articles in Scottish newspapers; all asking the question, *'Who was the Lady of Lawers?'* During the 1950s, when journalists reported on the Ben Lawers Hydroelectric scheme under construction at Finlarig, many wondered if the Lady had predicted the generation of power from water?

The decline in rural population and improving links saw the closure of Lawers School just after the end of the Second World War. The remaining seven pupils were transferred to the nearby school at Fearnan; severing one more link with the village's thriving past. Fearnan School itself closed in March 1968 and its ten pupils were moved to Kenmore School.

Who Was The Lady Of Lawers?

She made many prophecies.

A typical example is that a tree which she probably planted herself would grow near the church of Lawers and at various stages of its growth certain events of importance would happen.

When the tree reached the height of the gables of the church the Church of Scotland would be rent in twain. It was said that this stage corresponded with the Disruption in 1843.

When the tree reached the height of the ridge of the house of Balloch, Taymouth would be without an heir, which came to pass in 1862 when the second Marquis died.

That whoever cut down the tree would be sure to come to an evil end.

The tenant of a farm, along with a neighbour, had the temerity to put an axe to the tree. Other neighbours shook their heads with fear. The tenant was gored to death by his own bull and his helper lost his reason.

These facts are related by Rev. W. A. Gillies in his book, "Famed Breadalbane."

Many economic changes that have come to pass were foretold by the Lady.

She is said to have been a Stewart of Appin and the wife of one of the Lairds of Lawers.

But Mr Gillies says that this tradition conflicts with local family records.

He asserts there can be no doubt of the existence at the period of a lady gifted with a wonderful measure of wisdom and shrewdness and who was closely related to the Lairds of Lawers.

Some of her prophecies refer to the old Church of Lawers, now a ruined building. A stone over the doorway is dated 1669, which suggests she lived about the middle of the 17th century.

It is possible she was the wife of a younger brother of Sir James Campbell, the sixth laird, and that she resided in the house rebuilt after 1645.

According to local tradition the residence of the Lairds of Lawers was situated close to the water's edge a little distance to the west of the burn of Lawers, where the ruins of a double-storeyed thatched house still stand.

1948 newspaper article

When the National Trust of Scotland was granted stewardship of the site in the 1950s many were pleased that the resting place of Lochtayside's most famous resident would be protected from development and any further decay halted.

Small scale archeological studies were undertaken during the 1990s, during which some ceramics were found, together with some evidence of human habitation. The study, by the Archaeology Department of Glasgow University listed the probable buildings located in the village as follows:

"The Laird's House, Lawers Church (constructed 1669), two mills, nine other buildings, a corn-drying kiln, mill-lade, bridge, pier, a number of enclosures and a possible ice-house."

The NTS also undertook the cutting back of several blackthorn trees which were causing damage to the integrity of the site.

The site has been declared a protected site of special interest, and the potential for development is limited. It is sincerely hoped, however, that efforts can be made to clear away some of the fallen trees, roots and undergrowth which now obscure many of the buildings and have damaged some of the remaining walls. The deterioration, even in the past 20 or 30 years, is quite marked. TV presenter Tom Weir visited Lawers in an episode of *Weir's Way*, broadcast on STV in 1984. This programme is available on DVD, or to stream on youtube. Viewers can witness for themselves the damage caused by nature and neglect, even over this comparatively short period:

https://www.youtube.com/watch?v=yCBnLkrJgyo

In 1996 Aberfeldy solicitor David Ironside proposed an imaginative scheme to develop and preserve the site as a Heritage Centre. Mr Ironside lodged outline plans for 'The Lawers Experience' with Perth and Kinross Council for a visitor/heritage centre and tearoom. The scheme attracted support from Scottish Enterprise Tayside and tourism organisations, however the plans were eventually withdrawn.

There are many old and abandoned villages scattered around the highlands of Scotland, but few can compete with the atmospheric old village of Lawers. Its stories of mystery and genuine historical interest will beguile you. Indeed, in recent years visitors have unearthed trinkets from a bygone era, including an old iron pail and a hobnail boot! A visit will certainly fill you with wonder; and perhaps just an unnerving chill if you linger until the coming of darkness casts flickering shadows across the eerie ruins of a forgotten life.

Lawers was purchased by a private buyer in 2016. However, the new owner was unable to secure permission to build a new house on the site and, once again, the ancient village found itself on the market again in the summer of 2021. The sale attracted worldwide interest, featuring in news stories, websites and on social media all around the globe. The chance, it seems, to own a piece of Scotland with a resident ghost sparked enquiries from several countries! The author of this book was even asked to appear on television to discuss the fate of the abandoned settlement. Locals harboured genuine fears that the important historical site would, once again, be under threat of development. A local community buy out was even considered, however this would have required raising substantial funds.

Eventually, in September 2021 a private buyer from Glasgow became the latest owner in the near 1,000-year history of the village. The new owner hopes that, with the support of the local community, he can prevent any further degradation of the already tumbled down cottages. Together with a programme of weed and undergrowth clearance; coupled with the addition of interpretive signage, it is hoped that what remains of Lawers, can be preserved for future generations.

Perhaps, after a story lasting almost a millennium, this will not, after all, be the final chapter for this remarkable reminder of Scotland's past, sitting as it does, in a most beautiful and tranquil corner of Perthshire.

Lawers Cottage c1900
Building on the left believed to be Lawers Smiddy

Appendix A

I have attempted, where possible, to transcribe details of all those interred at the Cladh Machuim graveyard in Lawers. However, due to the spread of vegetation, inevitable weathering, and the passage of time, some information has now been lost. There are also several blank stones, from which no data could be gathered.

FIRST NAME	SURNAME	DETAILS	DATES IF AVAILABLE	AGE
Peter	Anderson		1878 - 1900	22
Peter	Anderson	Farmer near Killin Edramucky	1873 - 1960	87
Isabella	Bolton		1893	
Catherine	Browne		1926 - 1983	57
Annie	Calder	Nee Lawrence Black, Wife of walter	Monday, April 18, 1927	74
Walter	Calder	Minister of Lawers 1911 - 1925	Friday, March 26, 1937	85
John	Cameron	Tailor, Culltrannich	21 September 1876	47
Christina	Cameron	Nee McNab	Saturday, December 31, 1927	87

John	Cameron		November 14, 1900	34
Duncan	Cameron		1826	69
Ann	Cameron	Nee Campbell	1810	75
Duncan	Cameron	Son of Duncan and Ann	1851	26
Margaret	Campbell	Died at Machuim	24th February 1879	75
James	Campbell	Milton of Lawers	1799	
Margaret	Campbell	Nee Crearer	1822	
John	Campbell	Son of James	1866	52
Ann?	Campbell	Daughter of James	1818	
Alexander	Campbell	Justice of the Peace	1856 - 1930	74
John	Campbell		1886	52
Catherine	Campbell	Born 1824	25th August 1892	68
James	Campbell		1870	22
Colin Archibald	Campbell		1909	48
John	Campbell		1950	
Catherine	Campbell	Died in infancy	05 May 1953	0
Archibald	Campbell	Born 1768	March 1807	39
Elizabeth	Campbell	Nee Anderson		
Duncan	Campbell		1897	48
Donald	Campbell		1898	75
Peter	Campbell		1895	21
Duncan	Campbell		1930	
John	Campbell		1860	75
John	Campbell		1900	
Ann	Campbell		1865	

Robert	Campbell		Sunday, February 01, 1959	
Mary	Campbell	Nee Wright-Harvey, Wife of Robert	Tuesday, August 05, 1975	
Margaret	Campbell		Wednesday, December 19, 1923	59
Patrick	Campbell	Farmer and officer in First Breadalbane Battalion	1845	75
Christine	Campbell	Wife of Patrick	1862	73
James	Campbell	Farmer. Son of Patrick and Christine	1874	49
Jane	Campbell		1927	69
Duncan	Campbell	Perth, son of Jane	1968	78
D.	Clerk			
Margaret	Crearer		1882	
Peter	Crerar		27 May 1868	80
James	Crerar		21 October 1949	76
Anne	Crerar			
Christina Anne	Crerar	Died in infancy		
Christina	Crerar	Died in infancy		
Catherine	Crerar		1942	62
Jessie	Crerar			
Alexander	Crerar	F.R.C.S.	October 1860	60?

Grace	Crerar	Daughter of Alexander	Sunday, August 27, 1922	78
Margaret	Crerar	Daughter of Alexander	Sunday, April 24, 1955	60
James	Crerar		1948	75
Millie	Meredith	Wife of James Crerar	7/3/1969	79
Betsy	Dick		21 May 1905	69
Bessie	Dick	Wooden cross	1968	
James	Dixon		1940	66
Peter	Ferguson		1925	74
Doreen	Ferguson	Nee Campbell, wife of Peter		
Ann	Ferguson	McNab	1918	62
?	G		1731	
George	Hamilton		Monday, December 10, 1923	53
Jessie	Hamilton	Nee Cameron	30th October, 1942	65
George	Hamilton	Son of Jessie		
Donald	Hamilton	Son of Jessie	Friday, June 20, 1952	84
Donald Cameron	Hamilton	Son of Donald	Monday, August 19, 1957	49
Elizabeth	Hendry		Sunday, January 20, 1946	36
Matthew	Hendry		1969	?
Catherine	Know-Browne		1983	57

Malcolm	Lambie	Born in Killin	1907	5
?	M or E		1786	
D.	Mac?	Probably Daniel McAndrew, Forrester	1782	88
Donald	MacMartin	Died in infancy	1965	
Iain Peter	MacMartin	BSc Hons, PHD	1940 – 1973	33
John	MacMartin		1925	60
Peter	MacMartin		1826	61
Archibald	MacMartin		1890	75
Archibald	MacMartin	Reverened	1919	42
Peter Robertson	MacMartin		1930	
Mary Ann	MacMartin		1947	79
John Menzies	MacMartin		1957	
Elizabeth	MacMartin		1967	
John	Malloch		26 November 1807	80
Jessie	Malloch		1818	
Elizabeth	McCall	Nee McArthur, wife of Angus	Monday, October 01, 1923	84
Annie	McCall	Daughter of Angus	Monday, April 16, 1934	53
Matthew	McCall	Nephew of Duncan McCall	Tuesday, May 02, 1989	
Duncan	McCall		Sunday, May 26, 1957	75

Angus	McCall	Died at Croftintycan	Monday, October 09, 1922	83
Catherine	McCallum		1916	72
Margaret	McCallum		1915	51
Angus	McCallum		1939	67
Jessie	McCallum		1952	72
Elizabeth	McDiarmid	Nee Anderson	Sunday, October 12, 1930	67
Donald	McDiarmid	Husband of Elizabeth	Sunday, August 01, 1948	82
Duncan Anderson	McDiarmid	Son of Donald	Monday, January 28, 1957	54
Christina	McDiarmid	Daughter of Donald	Friday, September 26, 1975	74
Angus	McDiarmid	Son of Donald	Monday, October 10, 1988	80
Peter	McDiarmid	Drumglass, Lawers	Thursday, June 30, 1938	60
Margaret	McDiarmid	Nee McNab, wife of Peter	Saturday, February 12, 1955	73
Donald Campbell	McDiarmid			
Malcolm	McDiarmid		1915	85
Duncan	McDiarmid		1872	13
Donald	McDiarmid		1893	38
Peter	McDiarmid		1931	87
Jessie	McDiarmid		1839	63
Alexander	MacDonald	Died at Killin	12 August 1797	69

First Name	Surname	Details	Date	Age
John	McDougall	Farmer, Tullochcan Ardeonaig	Wednesday, December 03, 1924	68
John	McGibbon			
Peter	McGibbon	Son of John	May 1837	78
Peter	McGibbon	Corwhin	Tuesday, September 29, 1931	
Margaret	McGibbon	Nee MacLean, wife of Peter	Tuesday, May 16, 1922	
Catherine	McGibbon	Daughter of Peter and Margaret	Sunday, June 16, 1901	
Donald	McGibbon	Son of Peter and Margaret	Thursday, April 09, 1925	
Margaret	McGibbon	Daughter of Peter and Margaret	Tuesday, October 16, 1928	
John	McGibbon	Son of Peter and Margaret	Tuesday, January 07, 1936	
Ann	McGibbon	Daughter of Peter and Margaret	Saturday, June 11, 1955	
Christine	McGregor	Nee Campbell		
John	McGregor		1869	
Christina	McGregor	Daughter of John	1839	20
Archibald James	McGregor	Son of John	1820	3
Catherine	McIntyre	Nee Campbell	21 October 1880	72
Hugh	McIntyre	Husband of Catherine	27 September 1888	83

John	McIntyre	Son of Hugh	1 February 1878	24
Allan	MacKenzie	Minister of Lawers	Sunday, May 01, 1910	
Isabella	MacKenzie	Wife of Allan	Thursday, April 27, 1905	74
James	McLaren	Died at Lawers Toll	Sunday, September 04, 1955	88
Elizabeth Grant	McLaren	Nee Dunlop	Thursday, July 23, 1936	58
Peter	McLaren		1875	69
Janet	McLaren	Nee Robertson, wife of Peter	1908	87
Archibald	McLaren	Son of Peter and Janet	1876	
Janet	McLaren		1924	67
Janet	McLaren		Monday, December 30, 1946	69
Archibald	McLaren	Shepherd, Tullighglass, Ardtalnaig	21 February 1845	
James Archibald	McLaren	Son of Peter. Died in Melrose	Wednesday, May 27, 1992	
Margaret C.	McLaren	Died in Glasgow	Thursday, July 11, 2002	
Catherine	McMartin	Nee Cameron, wife of Malcolm	Friday, October 12, 1923	62

Malcolm	McMartin	Cuiltrannich	Saturday, August 02, 1941	78
Robert C.	McNab	Founder of Castle St. mission, Glasgow	Nov 1929 – Feb 19?	
Alexander	McNab		1835	
James	McNab	Farmer	1932	77
Mary	McNab	Passed away at Oban	Monday, January 27, 1919	72
Malcolm	McNab	Died at Creagan, Argyll	Saturday, January 18, 1936	95
John	McNab	Died in infancy, son of Malcolm and Mary		0
James	McNab	Son of Malcolm and Mary	17 September 1898	
Catherine	McNab	Daughter of Malcolm and Mary	Thursday, September 12, 1935	
Malcolm	McNab	Died in Bury St Edmunds	Wednesday, May 29, 2013	
Catherine	McNicol	Nee McIntyre	Sunday, January 27, 1901	63
Duncan	McNicol	Blacksmith	14 July 1892	72
Isabella	McNicol		August 1879	24
Margaret	McNicol		Thursday, May 15, 1919	51
Archibald	McNicol		Thursday, April 16, 1931	70

First Name	Surname	Notes	Date	Age
Mary	McNicol		Monday, November 02, 1931	75
John	McNicol		Tuesday, April 16, 1940	86
Betsy	McNicol		Monday, February 22, 1943	76
Duncan	McNicol		Wednesday, November 30, 1949	80
Malcolm	McNicol	Lived at Bankfoot	1891 – 1970	79
Peter	McPhail	Baluasuim	3 May 1872	72
Christian	McPhail	Daughter of Peter	20 February 1880	37
Duncan	McPhail	Son of Peter	13 April 1885	47
Elizabeth	McPhail	Nee McEwen	4 May 1889	85
William	McPherson	Private, Seaforth Highlanders	Sunday, May 22, 1921	33
Malcolm	McPherson		1922	37
Clementine	Reid	Nee MacMartin	Monday, July 25, 1966	59
Duncan	Robertson		1934	73
Euphemia	Robertson	Nee Cowan, wife of Duncan	1965	
Agnes	Robertson		1812 – 1904	92
Duncan	Robertson		2018	
Mary	Robertson		1918	79
Alexander	Robertson	Farmer, Croftintycam	Saturday, June 23, 1900	86

Janet	Robertson	Nee Campbell		82
Angus	Robertson	Son of Alexander and Janet		73
Jessie	Robertson	Daughter of Alexander and Janet		73
Archibald	Robertson	Son of Alexander and Janet		70
Donald	Robertson	Son of Alexander and Janet		
Alexander	Robertson	Ben Lowers Hotel	6-Oct-15	45
Janet	Robertson		14-Jan-77	66
Donald A.	Robertson	Buried at Killin		
Margaret	Stewart	Justice of the Peace	1982	78
?	W.M.		1531	
Alfred	Walker	Died in Glasgow	Saturday, May 01, 1943	
Jessie	Walker	Nee McNab, wife of Alfred	Thursday, March 04, 1965	
Mary	Walker	Daughter of Alfred and Jessie	Friday, April 15, 1988	
Margaret	Walker	Daughter of Alfred and Jessie	Tuesday, February 27, 1996	
Donald	Walker		1790	
John	Walker		1703	
Donald	Walker		Tuesday, November 29, 1904	

In addition, the following names are recorded on the War Memorial at Kenmore Church:

LAWERS

James McNab   Trooper, Scottish Horse

William Henry   Private, Black Watch

Peter McGregor   Private, Black Watch

Duncan McGregor Private, Black Watch

On the grave of the Revd. Allan MacKenzie is engraved the following inscription:

As a tribute of respect to

Revd. Allan MacKenzie, Minister of Lawers

Gus Am Bris An Là

(Translated from Gaelic as 'till the day breaks and the shadows flee away'. Taken from Solomon 4:6)

Appendix B

A STORY FROM
THE DUNDEE EVENING TELEGRAPH,
FRIDAY FEBRUARY 23RD 1894
'BREADALBANE FENCIBLE'S PROMISE:
A PERTHSHIRE STORY OF A CENTURY AGO.'

'John MacMartin, the subject of the following sketch, was born on the 1st of March 1767, at Cultrannich, Lawers, Lochtayside.

His father was the blacksmith of the district at that time and famed as a maker of swords and dirks all over the country, and if occasion required it is said that he was just as expert at handling them. John learned the same trade with his father, and it is said that he was no sooner master of his craft than he wished to become a soldier. This his father would not allow, as he was a good workman, and could still be wanted. However, an opportunity soon presented itself which neither father nor son could well refuse.

A number of young men were wanted to increase the strength of the Breadalbane Fencibles, and amongst the men billeted for the regiment was young MacMartin. For a few years everything went well with him, till in 1795 he found himself stationed with the regiment in Glasgow. Somehow at this time a serious disturbance broke out among the men. Their Highland natures could not bear the idea of corporal punishment, and a few of them having been committed to prison, and threatened with a sound flogging, a number of the regiment burst open the prison door and released the prisoners, thinking that by so doing the regiment would escape the disgrace of having any of their number flogged.

This action, of course, could not be overlooked by the authorities, and steps were taken to have the ringleaders punished. There being, however, so many concerned, it was no easy matter to fix on the real leaders. This difficulty, however, was got over by four of the men volunteering to become substitutes for the rest of the offenders, and endure the punishment for the offence. This mode of setting things right was accepted by the officers, and the four soldiers were conducted to Edinburgh, tried, and CONDEMNED TO BE SHOT. It was on the journey to Edinburgh that the interesting incident which we think worthy of recording occurred. MacMartin, who was one of the four men, stated to the officer in command that he knew what his fate was to be, but that he had left one very dear to him in Glasgow to whom he should like to say farewell. He knew that he was to die, and was willing to meet his fate, but death would be made easier to him by this, his last request, being granted. "A few hours," said he, "will do me altogether, and I will overtake you before you reach Edinburgh, and join you as your prisoner. "You, sir," he said to the leader, "

have known me since I was boy, and my father before me. You know Lawers and all my people. Believe me, I SHALL NEVER

BRING DISGRACE UPON YOU or my people by breaking my word of honour to you." The proposal was startling, and the responsibility great, but Major Colin Campbell, who commanded, knew the character of the soldier addressing him, and his fidelity to truth. The request was granted, and MacMartin was in Glasgow that night bidding his betrothed tender and final farewell. To keep his word he left Glasgow far behind by daybreak. He was hindered at times in his progress by keeping off the main road for fear of being taken up a deserter. These roundabouts took up so much of his time that when the hour specified arrived there was no appearance of him. Edinburgh was reached, but MacMartin had not appeared. Unable to delay any longer, the commander marched to the Castle with his prisoners, and was about to deliver them up, the same time deeply considering what he should say as to MacMartin's absence, At the very moment the poor fellow rushed up to his place in the ranks, glad that had not brought disgrace upon his kind-hearted officer, and that he had been able to make good is promise. He was sentenced along with the other three to be shot. This sentence was, however, revoked, and one only of the number was to suffer death. Lot deciding the victim, MacMartin was one of the three that escaped death. The victim was one William Sutherland, who was shot on Musselburgh Sands. MacMartin and his companions were banished to the Bermudas. What became of his companions afterwards is unknown; but MacMartin's sterling integrity and upright character in few years gained him his leave. He found his way to Canada, where, on the upper reaches of the St Lawrence River, he founded a small colony of raftsmen, and by 1820 this colony became a little village known *by the name of Martintown*. Referring to the above, James Cromb, in his "The Highlands and Highlanders of Scotland* (published in 1883)."

remarks— "This magnanimous self-devotion on the part of the poor Highlander is very striking indeed. It clearly shows how inviolable the Highlander considered his word, and what earnest regard he had for the safety of the man who had befriended him. Perhaps among men of honour this simple adhesion to promise—against all apparent interest—might not be accounted singular; but in this case it was the ignorant, low born peasant who allowed the grand instance of simple fidelity. It is pity indeed that his devotion was not accepted as sufficient atonement for the crime which his companions had so foolishly committed, and that the one victim was not spared, that he, too, might have shown some bright example of his gratitude and devotion to the service of his country.'

*The small settlement of Martintown still thrives near the St Lawrence River in eastern Ontario. A descendant of John MacMartin's, Alexander McMartin, became a businessman and political figure in Canada; becoming the first person born in Upper Canada to serve in its Legislative Assembly.

The family also established the Martintown Mill. After falling into disrepair the mill was purchased by descendants of the MacMartin family who donated it to Conservation Authorities.

A charitable organisation – The Martintown Mill Preservation Society – renovated the building and it is now open to the public as a museum. Similarly to the village of Lawers, the mill is rumoured to be haunted.

One cannot help but wonder how many of the inhabitants of Martintown realise that its very existence was only made possible by the unselfish act of one man from a now long-gone hamlet on the banks of Loch Tay.

APPENDIX C

The Castle of Lawers

Written by Lord William Graham, the 7th Earl of Monteith (born 1591 – died circa 1661). We can assume the story or legend below, at least in part, refers to the 50th birthday celebration of Sir James Campbell in 1623. Of particular interest are the only known references to the interior design of the original Lawers Castle and the land surrounding it. As the story provides confirmation that the castle was razed by the Duke of Montrose in 1645, it must have been written after that date. Interestingly, the final paragraph does not mention the construction of the new house, only the remaining castle ruins, meaning that the new house was probably not constructed at the time this story was first recorded (which must have been prior to Lord William Graham's death in around 1661). We do know that the new house was completed before 1664, however.

However, perhaps, most tantalizingly of all, is the (obviously romanticised and embellished) character of 'Lady Alice'. Did Lord William Graham actually meet the Lady of Lawers and perhaps base the character of Lady Alice on her? In fact, he may even have been related to her through his mother, Maria, who was a Glenorchy Campbell. His detailed knowledge of the castle seems to imply he was a regular visitor there; and we do know that the Lady of Lawers aroused the interest and fascination of many men, hence the constant presence of her protectors, 'The Companions'. If 'Lady Alice' was, indeed, inspired by The Lady of Lawers, then this story provides our only known description of her. It is an intriguing and enticing thought.

The Castle of Lawers was thought to have been lost for almost 200 years, until I unearthed the following version printed in the 1837 edition of *The Keepsake*, a little-known literary periodical which ceased trading in 1857.

I have provided some definitions of the more archaic word usage contained in this story at the end of the appendix.

'The feast was high in the ancient hall of Lawers; the chief of the Campbells had that day entered his fiftieth year, and his kinsmen and retainers from every part of the country were gathered together to celebrate Breadalbane's birth-day. Around the hall were hung the trophies of the chase and the triumphs of war. The noble antlers of the stag were crossed with the broad sword and the targe; while the casque and spear, and burnished breast plate, showed, that though in profound peace the chieftain was ever ready for the fight. In the middle, hung the broad banner of the Breadalbanes; and beneath, the escutcheon of their arms, with the proud and chivalric motto, "Follow me!"

The table in the centre of the hall groaned beneath the burden of the feast: at the upper end, on a seat of dais, sat the noble chieftain, with high features and commanding look; but, ever and anon, a dark scowl from his shaggy eyebrows seemed to tell that a Breadalbane never forgave an offence. However, generous in peace, and fortunate in war, his vassals followed willingly whithersoever he led. About him sat the ladies of his house, with fair hair and glancing eyes, bedecked with rich robes and precious stones, that glittered and shone in the flickering light of the blazing pine torches with which the hall was illuminated. But, one there was of surpassing beauty; her long sunny ringlets clustered on her graceful neck, which rivalled in whiteness the plumage of the ptarmigan, when the ground is covered with snow. Her blue eyes, as she gazed vacantly on the scene before her, poured forth a kind of dreamy light; but if aught said or done touched the latent feelings of her heart, the orbs suddenly expanded, and were lighted up with all the glow of enthusiasm, or of passionate indignation.

This was the Lady Alice, a cousin of the house of Breadalbane, and one who cared not to mingle too much in the gaieties and follies of the rest. For, most of all, did she delight to wander alone on the heathery mountains when the summer suns were setting in the west, and to linger and watch each departing ray, as it silently disappeared, like the vanishing hopes of glory. Sometimes, would she go forth when the spirit of the storm brooded on the hills; and, wrapping her mantle around her, listen to the groaning of the tempest and the rushing of the winds, till she returned with her hair and her dress all dripping with the out-pourings of its fury.

Often, would the Lord of Breadalbane chide her for these her wanderings, unbecoming, as he would say, in a noble lady. With that, would her eye glisten, her lips part as if to give utterance to the workings within; but anon, remembering the respect due to the head of her house, she would smother her rising feelings, and lower her head in token of feudal obedience.

In the evening, she again won back the chieftain's smile, by pouring forth her mellow voice in the songs of her native country, some spirit- stirring ballad of love and war; or almost melt even his iron nature to tears, by lingering, with melancholy strains, over some touching lament for the dead.

Such was the Lady Alice: but at the present moment she gazed upon the rude and boisterous scene with a vacant air, as if her thoughts were wandering far away from the festal board. Albeit, now did the feast become more joyous; rude and riotous grew the revelry at the lower end; toast upon toast was proposed and drunk, nor were the healths of the female part of the audience, and especially of the Lady Alice, forgotten. Many hearts throbbed at the mention of that name; for many were assembled in the hall that day who had been suitors for her hand. Nobles of high degree, barons, and chieftains, had wooed, but wooed in vain; to all, did she return a firm but dignified refusal, till her kinsfolk began to surmise she had made some vow of eternal chastity.

But they knew not her heart; her spirit was made for loving deeply, passionately, madly; yet, she could not devote her affections to beings who had no feelings in common with hers, who had no ideas beyond the best way of killing a stag or a man: and such were the only suitors that had as yet addressed her. In one of the pauses which occurred preparatory to the announcement of a new toast, a knock was heard at the door. The guests looked surprised, for none could come at such an hour, who intended to do honour either to the feast or the giver. Moreover, it was not the knock of one secure of admission by the haughty chieftain or impatient noble, but that of some humbler person, who hesitated as to the reception that might be awarded him. Breadalbane, however, motioned that they should see who was at the gate: the seneschal obeyed, and, soon returning, announced that there was without a young Irish harper, who craved admittance, that he might tell, in other lands, of Scottish halls and Scottish hospitality. His arrival could not have been more opportune; the feast was at its height, and all were ready to listen to the songs of the bard.

Breadalbane ordered him instantly to be admitted; the doors were thrown open, and all eyes were bent upon the stranger as he advanced slowly up the hall. He was partly wrapped in a large mantle, which disclosed a vest of green beneath; and a green cap, with a single feather, was placed upon his head. He appeared tall and handsome, and, casting around him a look of conscious mental superiority, he displayed more of the bearing of the noble knight than the humble harper. Such is, indeed, always the feeling of the true and loyal bard; he is proudly sensible of the dignity of his profession, and feels that, in the mental commonwealth, genius is the only legitimate sovereign.

The stranger strode to the upper end of the hall, where, doffing his cap and making an humble salute to the ladies and to the chieftain, he seemed to await their pleasure. Many were the fair eyes that were cast upon him, and none apparently with dislike or displeasure: his form and his face, his garb and his mien, were variously noted; and many were the guests that envied his lot when they saw the Lady Alice bend her large blue eyes upon him. After a short pause he addressed himself to Breadlalbane, and said that he was on his return to his native country; that he had visited many castles in his wanderings through Scotland, where he had been nobly entertained, but where ever he went the beauty of the Lady Alice was the universal theme; he had therefore bent his steps to the Castle of Lawers, in the hope that he might be able to carry back to his countrymen a true account of the fame of her beauty, and the hospitality of Breadalbane. A slight blush was seen by some to steal over the countenance of the Lady Alice during the harper's address,

"You are welcome, worthy harper", said the chieftain, "you are right welcome: you shall have the best entertainment my poor castle can afford , so shall we stand well in the eyes of other countries. As for my cousin Alice, Heaven has indeed been kind to her as to outward appearance, but whether her beauty shall prove a blessing or a curse, must be seen hereafter. However, you shall pledge me in this goblet, and anon we will have a trial of your skill in minstrelsy."

The harper quaffed of the goblet of wine, bowed to the ladies, and struck a few wild notes upon his harp.

"So please you, noble chieftain, shall it be a song of battle, or a lay of love?"

"In sooth", replied Breadalbane, "if I was to consult my own feelings and that of my knights, I should call for a song of battle, but as we have ladies present, we must allow them the choice; and if I interpret their looks aright, they incline to a lay of love."

The objects of his appeal all gave token of assent; the Lady Alice adding, "We are ourselves skilled in most of the minstrelsies of our own land. Perchance the noble harper has something from a far countree?"

"In sooth", replied the harper, "I have a ballad that tells of distant lands; but, methinks, that any bard would be unworthy of his art, whose tongue would not flow with unstudied lays, beneath the bright eyes that I see around me."

The Lady Alice was again observed to blush at these words, while the harper busied himself in arranging his chords, and recalling, as it were, by a few touches, the air and the words of his ballad. At last, the full tide of song broke upon him, and a deep silence being made, he commenced his theme.

When it was concluded, a general murmur of applause was heard throughout the hall. The Lady Alice was not slow in expressing her approbation, and it was generally agreed that the harper fully deserved to be rewarded with the poet's crown; the Lady Alice herself being appointed to place it on his brow. A wreath of evergreens was accordingly brought, and the harper was ordered to draw near, that he might receive the intended honour.

As he came forward and knelt at the foot of the dais, with bended head and downcast eyes, while the Lady Alice advanced, and the other damsels clustered around to witness the ceremony, the whole group would have made a subject worthy of the painter's brush.

None present observed that the hand of the Lady Alice trembled as she placed the wreath upon the harper's head; he alone felt it, and suddenly raising his eyes, he encountered those of the Lady Alice, which immediately fell, while a deep blush overspread her lovely face. Strange thoughts passed through the brain of the young harper; strange feelings rose in his breast; his blood beat rapidly in his veins; and hopes he did not dare to cherish, came and went, like misty stars through the stormy sky.

He was awakened from his trance by the voice of Breadalbane calling to him to rise, to pledge him in another goblet, and to drink a parting toast, "Good night to the ladies."

This was the signal for their retirement; and when he had caught the last glimpse of the Lady Alice, as she vanished through the lofty doorway; the harper also craved permission to withdraw. This was granted, and Breadalbane directed the seneschal to marshal him to his chamber, and to offer him the best entertainment the castle could afford. The rest of the company remained at the board.

The revelry waxed louder and more fierce, and many a dirk was drawn over the foaming goblet, which returned slowly and unwillingly to its sheath without its accustomed satisfaction of blood.

The iron bell of the castle had tolled many a chime beyond the hour of mid night, ere the wassail broke up and the guests wandered to their respective apartments. Strange and unaccustomed dreams haunted the pillow of the Lady Alice that night; slumber only sank upon her eyelids at intervals, ever and anon the image of the youthful harper flitted across her imagination, and new and indistinct feelings laboured in her bosom.

After this fashion passed the night; but with the early dawn she arose, feverish and unrefreshed, and having hastily donned her garments, she hurried into the garden to enjoy the cooling freshness of the morning air. She wandered along the broad walks, between the antique hedges of clipped yew, with her eyes fixed upon the ground, bewildered with the various thoughts which crowded on her brain, and with the new sensations which had suddenly arisen in her bosom. All at once she was awakened from her trance by hearing a few wild notes struck carelessly on a harp; she stopped, for she had not deemed that anyone would be abroad at this early hour except herself. In a few moments she recognized the voice of the harper, as he slowly chaunted the following verses:

> *Oh! I would wend with thee, love,*
> *Though all were night and sorrow,*
> *And I would die for thee, love,*
> *Though fate should say to -morrow.*
> *My cloak shall be thy couch, love,*
> *My arm shall be thy pillow,*
> *My sword shall be thy guard, love,*
> *O'er desert, mount, and billow.*
> *Then trust my heart and sword, love,*
> *My sword was ever true,*
> *And can you think my heart, love,*
> *Would e'er be false to you?*

As soon as the song was finished, she turned round to retrace her footsteps to the castle; she took, however, a path which led more directly to the house, than the one in which she had hitherto wandered. But in hastily turning the corner of one of the yew-tree hedges, she suddenly found herself in the presence of the minstrel.

His harp hung negligently on his arm, and his eyes were fixed upon the ground. Hearing footsteps he raised them, but on becoming aware of the presence of the Lady Alice, the colour mounted to his very temples. He soon, however, recovered his self-possession, and advancing towards her, he craved pardon for having thus intruded on the privacy of her matin walks,

"I did not conceive", he continued, "that anyone, much less the Lady Alice, would be abroad at such an hour; for myself, I must confess, that I love to greet the rising sun; there is something so delightful in the feeling and belief, that you are looking on a day that has, perhaps, not as yet been polluted by earthly sin, that I never feel myself so near to nature, and to nature's God, as at that early and untainted hour."

"That is indeed a sentiment," answered the Lady Alice, "worthy of the art and its master. But was the burthen of your early song, in sooth, a morning hymn?"

"A hymn, lady, to her I can never cease to worship, though I can never hope to approach her."

It was now the turn of the Lady Alice to look down and blush, as she encountered the ardent, though humble gaze of the youthful harper.

"Such was not the fate of the hero of your yester night's ballad."

"No, lady, no; but oh! How different are these things in fiction from actual life; but gladly, gladly would I undergo a thousand perils, to kneel but one hour at the feet of the angel I worship."

As he concluded these words, he struck passionately the chords of his harp, and then burst into the following strain:

> *I do not ask thee for thy love,*
> *A passing sigh is all*
> *That I can hope for, just to drop*
> *Within my cup of gall.*
> *And even that is more than I*
> *Can ask for as my due,*
> *I only ask in charity,*
> *And not for justice sue.*
> *I am not worthy of thy love,*
> *Nor can'st thou hope to find,*
> *Within the troubled mirror here,*
> *An image of thy mind.*
> *For how can innocence and guilt*
> *Together dwell below,*
> *Or how the nightshade and the rose*
> *Together bloom and blow.*
> *Farewell, farewell — I still must love,*
> *But will not cross thine eye,*
> *Forbear to curse me while I live,*
> *Forget me when I die.*

As he concluded these words he rushed hurriedly from her presence, and the Lady Alice, surprised, gratified, and yet, perhaps, slightly offended, returned slowly and ruminatingly to the gate of the castle. It is needless to say, that the resolution of the harper, as indicated by his song, was not kept; he still lingered about the castle, for Breadalbane still pressed him to stay, and offered him all the hospitality of the Scottish chieftain.

It is, perhaps, as needless to relate that interviews again occurred between the harper and the Lady Alice. She had at last found, what she long had sought in vain among the uncultured barons of the neighbourhood, a mind that corresponded with her own, in thought, word, and sentiment. She felt that their inward natures harmonized, though the outward forms and fashions of life had instituted an almost impassable barrier. Then began the struggle of conflicting passions; the self – sacrificing fervour of love, and the self-regarding principle of pride.

It was after one of these struggles with her contending emotions, struggles which had totally altered her nature, and changed the high and haughty, and apparently cold Lady Alice, into a being full of passionate ardour; it was, as I have stated, after one of these struggles, when the memory of her kinsman's proud castles, her ancient name and noble descent, had gradually yielded to the soft visions of mutual love, in some distant land, where the pride and the prejudice, the sin and the sorrow of the world should be alike forgotten , that she went forth one calm and beautiful evening to the accustomed tryste. The harper had prayed for one last interview, to bid an eternal farewell; for whether Breadalbane had observed anything which had excited his suspicions, or whether some envious spy had profaned the sanctity of their solitary meetings, however that might be, the Irish harper was no longer a welcome guest at the castle of Lawers.

The minstrel was true to his appointment. His face was pale, and his eye had a wild look of phrensy, as, taking the hand of the Lady Alice, and suddenly casting himself at her feet, he poured forth, with all the madness of despair, the utter hopelessness of his passion:

"Never", said he, "should the secret of my love have escaped from my lips, as long as I lingered here; but now, what is life to me – the star of my hope has fallen from the heavens, and the darkness of the idiot or the maniac will settle on my soul. Oh, that you were in my native land, amid the green hills and sequestered vallies of my own lovely country! Oh, that I could lead you to the hall of my fathers, and point out to you the tombs of all the noble bards of our race, bards who have won the crown of gold, and have received the worship of centuries! Would that my harp could win but one heart. But how can I hope to persuade you, lady, here within sight of Breadalbane's towers, and surrounded by all the power and the grandeur of a Highland chieftain. How can I hope to persuade you, that I, apparently an humble harper, am reverenced in mine own land. Yet so it is, lady, and I would not change the sympathising hearts that throng around the bard, for all the glory and the grandeur of the proudest earl in the land."

As he uttered these words his eyes flashed fire, and his whole face beamed with the light of enthusiasm; but soon again was his brow overcast, and again returned the look of despairing despondency,

"But what are the sympathising hearts to me? What the glory of my race, what the crown of gold? Why should I strive for honour or fame, when you, lady, cannot, or will not, share it with me? No, it is better that I seek out some desolate and lonely spot, where my grief shall be unheard, and my tears unseen; or if perchance some wandering shepherd shall catch the echo of my lamentations, he shall deem it but the murmur of the winds, or the wailing of some distant spirit."

He paused, for the sighs of the Lady Alice had now become quite audible; the tears coursed each other slowly down her cheeks, and her whole frame trembled with emotion, as if some mighty struggle was going on within. But no words escaped from her lips; a faint murmur now and then struggled forth, but her tongue refused to give utterance to the feelings of her breast. Suddenly, a death like paleness overspread her countenance, her limbs tottered, and she would have fallen had not the harper caught her in his arms, and gently placed her on a grassy bank.

How long she remained in this state she knew not; when she recovered her senses, the shades of night had closed around; lights glimmered in the distant windows of the castle, but all around the lovers was solitude and peace. Let us not disturb their last moments – let us not withdraw the pitying veil that night threw around them – let us not violate the sanctity of their parting interview.

The bell of the castle tolled at the usual hour the next morning, to summon the inmates to their early but substantial meal in the ancient hall. In a short time all had taken their seats in accustomed order at the well-filled board; but no sooner had Breadalbane entered, than he at once perceived that the Lady Alice was not in her usual place.

"Where is the Lady Alice?", he exclaimed, "let someone seek her in her chamber; perchance she still lingereth at her toilette, though it beseemeth that not young maidens to be too much addicted to their mirror. Eh, my fair ladies? Methinks, if they were all as faithful to their liege lords, as they are to their looking – glasses, we should hear of fewer broken vows."

The attendant returned and brought word, that the Lady Alice was not in her chamber; at the same time entered a groom, with the news that the palfrey of the Lady Alice was missing from its stall, although the night before it was fastened in the accustomed manner, and the stable door closed. The grim smile upon Breadalbane's face rapidly darkened into an ominous frown; he knit his shaggy eyebrows, and bit his nether lip till the blood started through the skin.

"Where is the harper?", he at last exclaimed, as he darted his fiery eyes around the room.

No one replied, and each person looked upon his neighbour, as it became evident that the harper had vanished also.

"Now, by the Holy Cross!", exclaimed Breadalbane, " 'tis as I suspected; and the cousin of our house has fled with this accursed harper! Truly, truly hath her beauty proved a curse instead of a blessing; but, by the light of heaven this insult shall not go unpunished! This accursed harper shall pay dearly for his presumption, and the vengeance I will take shall resound even unto his own land, and shall become a token and a warning to after ages. To horse, to horse, gentlemen; spare not the spur, rest not by day, sleep not by night, till ye have discovered the track of this accursed knave; and I will give my best charger, and broad lands upon the Tay, to him who first brings tidings of the traitor, dead or alive."

The castle was instantly all in commotion. Zeal inspired some, envy others, and vengeance for slighted vows quickened the ardour of not a few. The knights belted on their swords, the squires buckled on their spurs, and the grooms saddled their steeds. It was a gallant sight to behold, as they all mustered in the castle-yard, their spears glancing, their plumes waving, and their chargers neighing. In the midst of all, appeared Breadalbane on a coal-black steed, with a crimson feather dancing on his crest; giving his steed the spur, and crying out, "forward, gentlemen", with a scowling brow and glaring eye, he dashed out of the court-yard.

Each knight followed in succession, as waving his hand in adieu to the ladies, he vanished under the ponderous archway.

The sun was setting behind the lovely hills of Morven, as two travellers appeared upon the brow of one of the Argyleshire hills, which led down to the sea-coast, and which formed, as it were, the cape of that vast range of mountains, over which towered the shattered fork of Bencruachan, now lighted up by the dying rays of the declining sun. The landscape which spread around, was indeed worthy of being celebrated as the scene of Ossian's heroes; for seldom has pen or pencil pictured a more splendid assemblage of hill, and rock, and sea, and island, all blended and harmonized together by the glowing halo of a summer evening.

In the distance, stood the hills of Morven, with their lofty peaks, while at their base many a long and shadowy promontory jutted out into the golden sea. In the midground, on a projecting cape, rose the lofty towers of Dunstafriage Castle, mellowed into a rich purple colour, and which flung their softened shadows into the transparent waters below. On the right, jutted out the bold fronts of many a rocky headland, in the warm relief of sunset.

While, in the foreground, the gentle undulations of the sea broke in murmuring idleness on the gravelly beach.

The travellers, however, lingered not on the mountain's top, although their horses, apparently quite exhausted, tottered and stumbled adown the rugged path, while their haggard looks and disordered dress betokened that they had journeyed far, and tarried not for rest. One indeed, who from her dress was apparently a woman, seemed scarcely able to support herself in her saddle; for her companion, who was wrapt in a cloak, and displayed a green cap and feather on his head, rode close by her side, and seemed to support her with his arm , and encourage her with his words.

"Cheerily, cheerily, my beloved; see you not yonder, the bright waves dancing in the sun? Our task is almost over; we have reached the western coast; and once across the blue sea, the power, and the threats, and the rage of Breadalbane will be alike in vain. Look up, then, my beloved; let not your courage sink when within sight of the goal."

The object of his address did look up, but with such a pale and melancholy look, that the heart of the harper died within him.

"Alas, alas! Our efforts will be in vain; the hand of Fate is upon me, and its dark shadow has encompassed my soul. See you not those two ravens? They have followed us the whole way, over moor and moss, over hill and vale, by day and by night; even now they are whirling over our heads, and hoarsely croaking for their prey: they come not here for nothing. Again, last night, as we crossed over the brae of the mountain, the owl peered into our eyes as he flitted past, and I heard the wailing cry of the banshee as we hurried by the solitary cairn."

The harper continued, "Pri'thee cheer up, my beloved, and let not these melancholy thoughts oppress thee; let us think of the future, not of the past; the ravens are but gathered together for such chance relics as the sea may cast upon the shore, and it was but the wailing of the wind that thou didst hear in our midnight ride. The cool breeze of the evening hath chilled thy gentle form; let me wrap my cloak around thee, and shield thee from the falling dew."

He undid his mantle, and proceeded to wrap it around her trembling frame; while he was busied in this operation, he suddenly felt all her body cower together, as if with some violent convulsion, while a sharp scream burst from her lips.

"Ah! Look, see there, see there!", the Lady uttered, with her goodly gift of vision, "on the top of that hill a spear glanced in the setting sun."

He looked up, and beheld indeed what his worst fears had foreboded; on the brow of the hill he saw a horseman stand in dark relief against the sky; he appeared to be scanning the horizon round and round. For a moment the harper indulged the hope that he might escape the ken of his searching eye; but suddenly the horseman appeared to gaze steadfastly into the valley below, then making a sign, as if to some one behind, he dashed down the side of the mountain, and was presently lost to sight. With a vain hope, the harper dashed the spurs into his steed, and seizing his companion's palfrey by the bridle, urged the horses to one more effort. The faithful creatures responded to his call; they seemed as if they almost knew that life or death depended on their speed, and for some few paces they appeared to have recovered all their pristine vigour. But this preternatural exertion could not last: in galloping along the rugged path, a loose stone rolled from beneath the foot of the lady's palfrey; the poor animal stumbled, made a vain effort to recover his footing, and failing, fell with his exhausted burden to the ground. In the agony of his despair, the harper jumped from his horse, threw his arms around the Lady Alice, for such she was, and entreated her by all the endearing names that a lover could devise, to make but one more effort. The Lady Alice slowly opened her eyes; she was but slightly stunned by the fall, and the harper taking her in his arms, and folding her to his breast, hurried with all the speed and strength he could exert, towards the sea shore.

He saw a solitary fishing-boat lying on the sand, and if he could but reach that, all might yet be well. But, alas, his enemies were now closing upon him: other horsemen had appeared upon the hill, and the one who had first dashed down the mountain's side, now emerged upon the heath, and was but a short distance in their rear. The red plume of Breadalbane streaming in the wind, told but too plainly that their bitterest foe was foremost in the chase. Escape appeared impossible; every moment brought his enemy nearer, and with a look of despair, the harper placed his lovely burthen on the ground, and drawing his sword, prepared to defend his charge to the last moment of his existence.

In a few moments the foremost horseman reached the fugitives; he dismounted, cast his steed loose, drew his sword, and crying out

"Ha, traitor! Have I caught thee?", rushed upon the unfortunate harper. The tall, slender, and graceful form of the latter was but ill-fitted to contend in mortal strife with the strong, stern, iron-armed, and iron-hearted chief of Breadalbane. But at the first clash of their swords, the Lady Alice started from her trance, and seeing her lover engaged in deadly fight, without a moment's thought or hesitation rushed between the combatants. For a moment the strife was stayed, for even the iron heart of Breadalbane was softened, as he saw his beautiful kinswoman throw herself across the body of the harper, she exclaimed, "Now, then, strike!"

But Breadalbane's fury soon returned, and seizing her by the waist, with the assistance of his attendants, who were now come up, he tore her from the arms of her despairing lover. The rest may be quickly told: the harper soon fell beneath the blows of his assailants, and in the fury of the moment, his body was literally cut to pieces. In the agony of her despair, the Lady Alice had fainted; but when the pulse of life again returned, and she saw the miserable remnants of what had once been her lover, the light of her mind fled for ever, and she sank into a state of hopeless melancholy.

In this state, she was carried back to the castle. Breadalbane, when the fury of his passion was over, and his vengeance satisfied, lamented the wreck he had made; for with all his sternness and fierceness, he had really loved the Lady Alice. Every means were tried to restore her to health; every indulgence granted, every fancy gratified; but the only thing in which she appeared to take any delight, was to wander about alone in the garden of the castle, to linger in those spots where she first met the harper, and to sit, as the sun set and the moon rose, under that fatal bower where the first avowal of love burst from his burning lips.

In this condition, she lingered a few months, gradually wasting away, like a perishing flower, till one evening, as the attendants of the castle were seeking for her in order to lead her home, the hour growing late, they found her lying cold and lifeless in her favourite spot. The fate of the harper was not forgotten by his countrymen.

Many years afterwards, when the Irish auxiliaries came over to Scotland to assist Montrose in his chivalrous but unfortunate enterprise, a small band detached themselves from his standard during one of his irruptions through Perthshire. They marched under a chief of their own, and making for Breadalbane's country, they arrived at nightfall before the Castle of Lawers. Not expecting any attack, the chieftain was absent; the small garrison was taken by surprise, and every soul put to the sword. The castle itself was fired, and its walls razed to the ground; and the desolate ruins remain to this day a lasting memorial of Breadalbane's fury and of Irish revenge.'

Targe – Shield

Casque – Helmet

Burnished – Polished

Escutcheon – Shield or emblem bearing a coat of arms

Dias – A platform on which a throne sat Vassal – Someone granted land by a Lord in return for homage and allegiance

Mantle – A long, sleeveless cloak

Seneschal – The steward of a large medieval house Mien – A person's appearance or manner Dirk – Short dagger, traditionally carried by Highlanders Wassail – A hearty and noisy drinking celebration Burthen – An archaic form of the word burden Cup of Gall – An outrageous affrontery, to ask for something beyond your expectations

Phrensy – Archaic spelling of frenzy

Palfrey – A docile horse, usually reserved for female use Ossian – A reference to the Gaelic warrior-poet Oisín Betokened – To display an indication or sign Tarried – to delay, or stay longer than intended Pri'thee – An ancient form of please, used to convey a request

Ken – Vision, understanding or knowledge Irruption – A sudden, violent or forcible entry *The Castle of Lawers* is an extraordinary tale. Whilst, obviously embellished for the romantic Victorian fiction market, the story contains elements that provide us with the first known description of the original tower house at Lawers, together with its gardens. The swords and shields, the armour, the dining hall, the pine torches, the yew trees, and the iron bell, offer us an evocative description of life in the Castle of Lawers in the early 1600s.

The enigmatic character of 'Lady Alice' presents us with an intriguing question too. Is she really 'The Lady of Lawers'?

Several parallels appear to indicate so. Firstly, the impression of a lady 'abroad' (meaning away from familiar lands and her own people, in this context). Secondly, the character of the Harper seems to provide a strong metaphor for the Campbells' suspicion and fear of both the Irish and the Stewarts of Appin, no doubt engendered by their support of Montrose's Army.

Following the razing of the castle and chapel by Montrose (aided by his Irish support) in 1645, the fear proved to be a justifiable and wholly real one.

Then why change the name of the character to 'Alice'?

Perhaps, in writing this story, it is conceivable that Lord William Graham may have wished to safeguard the Lady from any Campbell vengeance, which her Stewart blood might have provoked? Or perhaps he intended to protect from the remaining vestiges of the Scottish witch hunts. There certainly does not appear to have been a Campbell named Alice recorded at that time.

Yet, the parallels do not end there. The character of Lady Alice seems wistful and melancholy, as she wanders the countryside. She becomes restless as a result of troubling dreams – perhaps a metaphor for The Lady's visions? Lady Alice enjoyed the company of a companion from home. Earlier in this book I refer to 'The Companions' who accompanied The Lady on her arrival at Lawers. The character of the Harper seems to suggest a similar theme.

The legend of The Lady of the Lawers also tells us of her favourite ash tree which she planted; and which, underneath, she buried her much loved companion from home. Similarly, *The Castle of Lawers* informs us that Lady Alice sat *'under that fatal bower where the first avowal of love burst from his burning lips.'*

The Lady Alice is described as 'not a young maiden', which The Lady of Lawers would certainly not have been at the time of William Graham's visits to Lawers. It is likely she was at least 35 years of age by the mid-1640s. According to this story, the menfolk at the Castle of Lawers all seem to possess a lingering fascination and attraction to her. If the Lady of Lawers' husband had indeed been killed at the Battle of Auldearn in May 1645, and she was as beautiful as she is described here, then it is entirely plausible that she would have aroused the interest of the men attending the feast that night.

Possibly, however, the most tantalizing clue in the story is the mention of her 'goodly gift of vision'. Assuming this is a thinly veiled reference to the Lady of Lawers, then it seems to confirm that her abilities as a 'Seer' were known before her prophecy referring to the ridging stones at Lawers' Church in 1669. Perhaps any prophecies she made before that date where not believed, or possibly ridiculed? Or, more probably, were either not recorded, or have simply been lost in the mists of time.

Perhaps we will never know the truth behind the enigmatic Lady of Lawers, but I sincerely hope *The Lost Village of Lawers* and my rediscovery of *The Castle of Lawers* help to explain her enduring mystery and appeal even in this more cynical and scientific age.

Lord William Graham

Appendix D

Finding The Lady

The prophecies pronounced by the Lady of Lawers have survived intact for more than three centuries, but do any physical traces remain in the village that can still offer us a tantalising clue to the existence of the Lady herself? Did she really exist? And if she did, what evidence of her remarkable abilities can we still locate?

Surprisingly, even after more than 300 years, the eagle-eyed visitor may still find some clues.

The first hint at the presence of an important seer in the village is probably missed by all those who walk down the track towards Lawers. As you approach the gated entrance to the village, on the steepest part of the path, the passer-by will notice the presence of several Rowan trees deliberately planted alongside the tumbling and ancient drystone walls that border the track. Rowan trees hold an important place in Scottish Celtic mythology. They are believed to possess several special powers, all of which provide us with an important link to the extraordinary reverence in which the Lady of Lawers was held by those in the village. Rowan trees were often planted at the approach or entrance to a village or home to offer protection against witchcraft, unwanted visitors or invaders. Even to the extent that weapons fashioned from the wood of the Rowan tree were said to possess magical powers. Perhaps they were planted to discourage further attacks (following the razing of the village by the Duke of Montrose in 1645), or against the ferocity of the witch hunters?

The presence of Rowan Trees was also said to ward off evil spirits, so feasibly their planting may even have been masterminded by the Lady herself, as protection against the misfortune she foresaw. The berries of the tree have significance in many cultures for two reasons. Firstly, for their red colouring, which can be traced back from Celtic tradition, through Norse folklore, to ancient Greek mythology, in which the gods dispatched an eagle to battle the evil spirits who had stolen the magical cup of the gods. It was believed that a Rowan tree would grow at the precise spot that a drop of blood or a feather from that eagle fell to earth. This sacrifice by the eagle was thought to give the Rowan tree its feathery leaves and round blood red berries.

The five-pointed outline visible on the surface of the berries was thought to offer a shield from evil spirits or bad omens. The configuration of this shape was considered, according to Celtic tradition, to offer the same protection as the five-pointed pentangle in ancient religion, predating even the cross.

Interestingly, the Rowan tree was more commonly known by other names during the 16th and 17th centuries – the Mountain Ash, the Wild Ash, the Wicken, the Witches' Tree, Witchbane, Witchwood, the Lady of the Mountain, the Enchantress of the Woods, the Tree of Light and the Tree of Stars. These names all seem to offer us yet another enticing hint at the presence of a person with special powers within the village. In fact, the name 'Mountain Ash' was often used to describe Rowan trees because they were planted on mountainsides and hills within the Highlands, as it was believed that the nearer the trees were planted to the sky, the greater their connectivity to the 'Otherworld' (the Celtic supernatural or parallel universe inhabited by the chosen few who possessed unearthly powers. It was an existence in which only they could crossover or were able to envisage). The Rowan tree was thought to be the most powerful conduit between this world and the other.

The presence of the Rowan trees at Lawers and on the nearby hillsides may explain the Lady of Lawers' fascination with Ben Lawers and its inclusion as a point of reference within several of her prophecies.

In ancient Celtic culture the Rowan tree was named 'li sula' (the colour of vision) thought to relate to its visionary properties. Ancient druids also used the smoke of burning Rowan wood to conjure up the Otherworld and divinatory foresights.

Perhaps, the existence of the mystical Rowan tree within the old village of Lawers may also offer us a more in depth understanding of her most well-known prophecy.

'T *high sgiorradh obann air an duine a ghearras a chraoibh.*'

(A sudden accident will befall the man who cuts down the ash tree).

This prophecy reputedly referred to the ash tree planted by the Lady adjacent to the church. According to legend, the Lady buried her much loved companion beneath the tree; and was possibly buried there herself. However, the 'ash' tree referred to in the prophecy may well have been a Rowan Tree (a 'mountain ash'), which, with its symbolic connotations, seems a far more likely tree to have been chosen. In Celtic mythology it was believed that a body planted beneath the roots of a Rowan tree would be 'staked to the earth', with the sacred tree easing the passing of the recently departed and preventing their ghostly spirit from walking the earth in eternity. Perhaps this explains the Lady's stern warning, forbidding anyone from felling the tree? Interestingly, despite her mystical reputation, I was unable to trace any stories reporting visions of her ghost, that pre-date the removal of her tree in 1875.

In addition, the growth rate and life expectancy of a Rowan Tree – no more than 30cm per year – seems to fit the time period in which *the tree grew to the gable height of the church* (according to the Lady's next prediction), and the fact that she placed a curse upon anyone who would cut it down. Perhaps the unfortunate John Campbell, who felled the tree in 1875, was merely being a judicious tree surgeon. By 1875 the tree would have reached the end of its natural life cycle and may well have been dangerous. Sadly, for John Campbell, he did not live long enough to leave behind an explanation for his decision to chop down the Lady's much-loved tree.

Should one choose to interpret the folklore and tradition of Scottish Seers, there are other, more subtle, hints at the Lady's possible residence at the House of Lawers to be divined from a visit to the old village. The exact positioning of her house is in marked contrast to the nearest two dwellings, which both sit at a 90-degree angle to the Lady's home. Perhaps, in line with Celtic tradition, the Lady needed a view of the water and, with it, its conductive powers for those gifted with the ability of second sight. There are no windows on the gable ends of the Lady's house, only on the side facing the water. During the 17th century, the level of Loch Tay was slightly higher than it appears today, and the foreground much less overgrown, affording the Lady an uninterrupted view of the water. Her home, as the castle did before it, sit just as few feet from the bank. Perhaps she required this to assist her visionary abilities? Celtic folklore informs us that the Seer needed to be next to water, to acquire wisdom through seeing her own image reflected in the water.

The position of the graveyard and the Machuim Stone Circle predate the arrival of the Lady of Lawers at the village. However, they undeniably hold a mystic significance in Gaelic culture. Perhaps these ancient places also held some significance for her? Long before the village existed, or the modern road, the plain of Machuim extended from the stone circle down to the water's edge. Once much larger, the stone circle has existed for probably 3,000 years. Although its original purpose is unknown, it is generally believed that Celtic stone circles held religious or spiritual significance and possibly assisted as an amplifier for those connecting with the Otherworld. Although now mostly overgrown and collapsed, visitors to the circle reported hearing voices and an unearthly presence during the Victorian era.

An alternative version of the Lady's death states that she is buried at the entrance to the graveyard at Lawers. There is little evidence to substantiate this. Nevertheless, there is a hidden gravestone (in an undisclosed location) which contains, what appears to be a sideways letter 'M'. The letter is deliberately placed at a 90-degree angle to the date and is similar to the witches' marks often found carved into the walls and beams of known witches or soothsayers houses during the 17th century.

On a personal level, on my frequent visits to the graveyard during my research for this book, I always encounter the same unsettling experience. Despite the abandoned village being fairly remote, I always receive a perfect 4G mobile phone signal there – except for the exact moment I step into the graveyard. The signal disappears completely, along with any phone reception, only to miraculously reappear the moment I step out again. Very disconcerting!

Finally, the Lady of Lawer's often used sheep as a metaphor in her prophecies. Sheep were farmed in Lawers even before the Highland clearances; and were certainly plentiful during the Lady's lifetime. In Scottish Celtic tradition the shoulder-bone of the sheep was used as a prophesising tool, which assisted in the seer's connection with the Otherworld. First the bone needed to be cleaned, but iron could not be used to scrape any meat from the bone. Therefore, the presence of water must have been invaluable!

Each point mentioned here and throughout this book, taken individually, hint at the suitability of Lawers as a safe and fruitful place for a seer to make their home. However, taken in unison, it is undeniable that the ancient village of Lawers seemed to offer the perfect conditions for a visionary – in the great Celtic tradition – to flourish.

It remains a tantalising and enigmatic mystery. A visit to the remains of Lawers will doubtless leave you pondering the question. As daylight fades among the ruins and the sun sets to the west, twilight is transformed into the inky blackness of the night. Perhaps, only then, can answers be found. For it is always at that time that her spirit is reported to be still wandering the village that she made her home more than 350 years ago. Indeed, as recently as 2006, workmen staying at the local hotel reported a disturbing presence whilst working at the village; coupled with an uneasy feeling of being watched.

There is an even more detailed sighting, which occurred during the 1970s, and is recorded in the book *Scottish Hauntings* by Grant Campbell.

An experienced hillwalker named Gwyn from Wrexham in North Wales was holidaying in the Scotland and had decided to walk from Killin to Lawers along the northern shores of Loch Tay, in the hope of visiting the Lady of Lawer's grave in the ruins of the old village. It had been a warm and muggy June day. Around 8:00pm he reached Lawers, having walked in the sun all day. He decided to find a sheltered spot to rest and to camp for the night.

In a field, close to the ruins of old Lawers Gwyn found a suitable spot and pitched his tent for the night. Close by, stood the remains of the Lady's house. The building was empty and quiet, as was the nearby loch. Then, suddenly, in the stillness of the night he heard the distinct sound of a thud coming from the ruins of the house. He jumped up, frightened, but decided he would investigate. During midsummer in the Highlands, the light remains until well after 11:00pm and there was still enough light to see without a torch. As he approached the doorway of the empty tumbledown property, he was overtaken by a strange, unexplained, and compelling urge to call out in Scottish Gaelic. Yet Gwyn had no knowledge of the language. As he peered into the shell of the empty room there was complete and utter silence. Yet in the shadows of the far corner a group of three or four women suddenly materialised. They appeared to be gathered around a table, hunched over, their backs to the doorway. Each of the women was dressed in dark clothing, with a large shawl draped over their heads and shoulders. Their clothing was not modern, it seemed to belong to a different time. They did not see him enter, and continued with whatever task was occupying them.

He attempted to speak, but could not. As he tried in vain to talk, one of the group turned around so that her face was visible. Although she did not appear to notice Gwyn, he was able to see that she was young - no more than sixteen years old. Her hair was long and fair, the tresses emerging from underneath her shawl, and she appeared to be smiling.

At that exact moment, the figure of a tall, thickset man suddenly appeared, seemingly from the stone wall to the right. He was dressed in a baggy white shirt and dark red kilt with yellow stripes. The man bent down, as if to warm himself by the disused stone fireplace. He then strode purposefully towards the centre of the room before vanishing in front of Gwyn's eyes.

Still Gwyn's presence did not seem to have been noticed by the occupants of the room. Just as the man in the kilt disappeared, the figures of two more men suddenly appeared in the room. Where they had come from, Gwyn could not tell. Yet these men were somehow different. Their clothing appeared to be from a different era altogether. Grey suits and cloth caps, perhaps the fashion of the 1920s, he thought.
Then, still unable to speak or interact, the whole scene vanished before his eyes. He was quite alone again. The whole incident had lasted no more than two or three minutes.

Frightened and stunned by what he had seen, Gwyn dared not venture any further into the room. Instead, he turned and left hastily, gathering his possessions as he ran. Once he was a safe distance from the ruins of the abandoned house, he spent the night sheltering in the outbuildings of a farm.

He was never able to find the Lady of Lawers' grave, but the memory of what he did witness that night remained with him for many years. He typed his vivid experience on several sheets of paper, recording every strange detail.

One of the many Rowan Trees at Lawers

Appendix E

Census and Kirk Records

For this latest edition of The Lost Village of Lawers, and in addition to those names listed in Appendix A, I have been able to unearth details of the following families known to have been resident in Lawers prior to the abandonment of the village.

In several cases, despite Kirk records listing the burial of the names below within the graveyard at Lawers, these individual's gravestones are sadly no longer visible – possibly destroyed, now completely overgrown, and buried under centuries of undergrowth, or worn by the passage of time.

It is important, nevertheless, in helping to build as complete a record as possible of life within the ancient community of Lawers.

Anne Anderson born 1772 died 1827 Aged 55

Christina Anderson born 1789 died 1859 nee Stewart, died aged 70

Donald Anderson born 1775 died 1860 Aged 85

Duncan Anderson born 1768 died 1855 Aged 87

John Cameron born 1786 Forester Son of Duncan Cameron and Ann Campbell

Donald Cameron born 1908 died 1957 Aged 49

Donald Cameron born 1868 died 1952 Aged 84

Ann Campbell born 1765 died 1840 Aged 75

Alexander Campbell born 1825 died 1854 Aged 29

James Campbell born 1748 died 1799 Tackman, Milton Lawers. Wife – Margaret

Archibald Campbell born 1807 died 1840 Aged 33

Christian Campbell born 1866 died 1866 *Twins, died in infancy, unmarked grave*

Elizabeth Campbell born 1866 died 1866 Twins, died in infancy, unmarked grave

Christian Campbell born 1790 died 1862 Aged 72

Duncan Campbell born 1729 died 1796 Aged 67. Third son of Archibald Campbell

Doreen Campbell born 1949 died 1949 Died in infancy

Gillespig Campbell born ? died 1859

James Campbell born 1779 died 1865 11 May 1865. Aged 86

James Campbell born 1825 died 1874 Aged 49

James Campbell born 1822 died 1841 Aged 19

Lillias Campbell born 1831 died 1841 Aged 10

Janet Carmichel born 1822 died 1891 Aged 69. Erected by sons John and Duncan

Duncan Combich* born ? died ?

Christian Crerar born 1826 ? Listed as farmer, Mill of Lawer

Majory Crerar born ? died 1780

Margaret Crerar born 1822 Wife of James Campbell

James Dewar born 1720 died 1805 Tenant of Drumglas at Lawers

Duncan Dior born ? died 1741 Drumglass

Jessie Dixon born 1876 died 1939 Died at Monkton. Aged 62

John Ferguson born 1814 died 1882 Aged 68

Catherine Grahame born 1786 died ? Tenant of Mill of Lawers

Malcolm MacGregor born ? died 1828

Catherine Malloch born 1821 died 1884 Aged 63

Cumruich Mann born ? died 1834 Married to Catherine McIntyre in 1764

John Mann born 1735 died 1829 Aged 94

Margaret Mann born 1729 died 1814 Aged 85. Wife of James Dewar, Drumglas

Daniel McAndrew born 1724 died 1782 Aged 58. Sons also buried at Lawers

Francis MacGibbon born ? died 1847 Died at Killin

John MacGibbon born ? died 1847

Catherine McGregor born 1783 died 1859 Aged 76

Christian McGregor born 1819 died 1839 Aged 20

Donald McGregor born ? died 1806 "Buried under turf"

John McGregor born ? died 1865 also known as John McGreach

Margaret McGregor born 1757 died 1820 Aged 63. Third wife of John Mann

Katherine McIntosh born ? died 1770 Wife of John Anderson, Carpenter

Catherine McIntyre born ? died 1764 First wife of John Mann

Catherine McLaren born ? died 1786 Second wife of John Mann

Donald MacMartin born 1813 died 1884 Aged 71

Duncan MacMartin born 1805 died 1830 Died 20 August 1830, Aged 25

John MacMartin born 1805 died 1846 Aged 41

Robert MacMartin born 180 died 1875 Aged 74

Elizabeth McMartin born 1823 died 1891 nee Anderson, died aged 68

Janet McMartin born 1803 died 1883 nee Carmichael, died aged 80

Christina McNab born 1778 died 1855 Aged 77

James McNab born 1855 died 1932 Aged 77

Angus Stewart born ? died ? Husband of Catherine Stewart

Catherine Stewart born 1767 died 1855 born at Balnasuim, Lawers. Died aged 87

Clementina Stewart born 1835 died 1916 Aged 81

John Walker born ? died 1795

Mary Benskin born 1787 died 1863 Aged 75

Duncan Cameron born ? died ? Teacher and Baptist Minister

John Cameron born 1830 died ?

? Campbell born ? died 1877

Arthur Sibbald Grieve born ? died 1881

The following people were also born in Lawers, but subsequently moved away and are not interred there:

Annie MacPherson born 1873 moved to Stoke-on-Trent

John McCallum born 1856 moved to Merton, Surrey

Helen Fitzgerald born 1861 moved to Willesden, Middlesex

John MacDonald born 1884 moved to Islington, London

Alexander MacDonald born 1885 moved to Islington, London

*It appears that those bearing the name Combich (later to be anglicized to Stewart) first moved to the area from Appin, probably with the Lady of Lawers. Over the next 100 years a substantial number appear on the Kirk records for Killin and Kenmore. Duncan Combich (listed above) appears to be the first Combich (Gaelic for guardian or companion) recorded in the Lawers area.

A study of the Kirk Session records at Kenmore Church Further adds further credence to this version of the Lady's heritage. Session records indicate the arrival of the Combich Stewarts from Appin in Argyll at the Milton of Lawers by the middle of the 17th century. A 1923 editorial in the Perthshire Advertiser reported on the long held local tradition linking the arrival of the Combich Stewarts on Lochtayside with the arrival of the Lady. It was assumed that the first of the Stewarts to make their home at Lawers were the escorts and bodyguards of the Lady of Lawers. The earliest known recorded individual seems to have been Duncan Combich; perhaps he was the Lady's first protector?

Many Stewarts in the area can still recall ancestors using the surname Combich or Combaich, however the Gaelic spelling seems to have died out by around 1850.

Appendix F
The Ferryman's Cottage

The watercolour may have been painted around the time that Hugh McDiarmid was ferryman at Lawers. A flowery description of the Ferry House appeared alongside a photograph of the watercolour in the *Glasgow Weekly Herald*, 27 July 1912

'Our sketch is taken from a watercolour drawing and shows the ancient Ferry House of Lawers, on Loch Tay. The group is typically Highland in character, with its thatched roofing, low walls, and obviously primitive stonework.

For centuries the Ferry of Lawers was one of the most important on Loch Tay, and travellers going south were wont to cross the loch at this point for

Ardtalnaig and the wild hill paths leading past Innergeldie to Comrie and the Lowlands.

The Ferry House is beautifully situated. It stands on a slightly raised grassy terrace where the crystal waters of the burn of Lawers enter the loch after their brief but turbulent journey from Lochan a Chait (the 'Loch of the Cat'), which lies, dark and deep, amid the precipitous solitudes of Ben Lawers. Embowered in roses and all manner of summer flowers, the Ferry House, with its clean whitewashed walls and warmly tinted, cosy-looking thatch, presents a rare scene of quiet sylvan beauty.

The bosky little glen through which the burn tumbles on its way to the loch forms a picturesque setting for the watercolour. A century ago the Ferry House was the centre of a flourishing hamlet. We may still trace, in the ruined grass-grown wall and mossy mound, the scenes of a vanished life, but "the hare kittles on the hearthstones" and wild briar and wandering fir grow now in luxurious profusion where the children of long ago were wont to play.

But the life that once ebbed and flowed around the old Ferry House has melted into the distant past. Its memories, however, continue to haunt the spot, and if perchance the passing rambler foregathers with the ancient ferryman or his respected better half he may learn – if he cares – much of the store of tradition and legend that lingers around Loch Tay.

The Ferry House is said to be the oldest house in Breadalbane, and, judging by its venerable appearance, we are quite prepared to accept the statement. Whether it be the oldest or not matters little. One fact is clear. It is certainly the centrepiece of one of the bonniest spots in Breadalbane, and in historic interest it yields to few. It is an ideal haunt of ancient peace, a place of memories, where naught breaks the stillness but the soft murmur of the loch as it gently kisses the silver strand. Over everything, broods the majestic bulk of Ben Lawers the Gaelic "mountain of the new day", itself the very embodiment of the spirit of the ages whom "The new day is only now at the dawn."

Across the burn from the Ferry House is the old kirkyard – "girt with the lumber of the hamlet's dead", where the soft hand of time has spread a mantle atop the sombre silent graves.'

Ferryman's Cottage, Lawers (Cladh Machuim Graveyard is visible in the background)

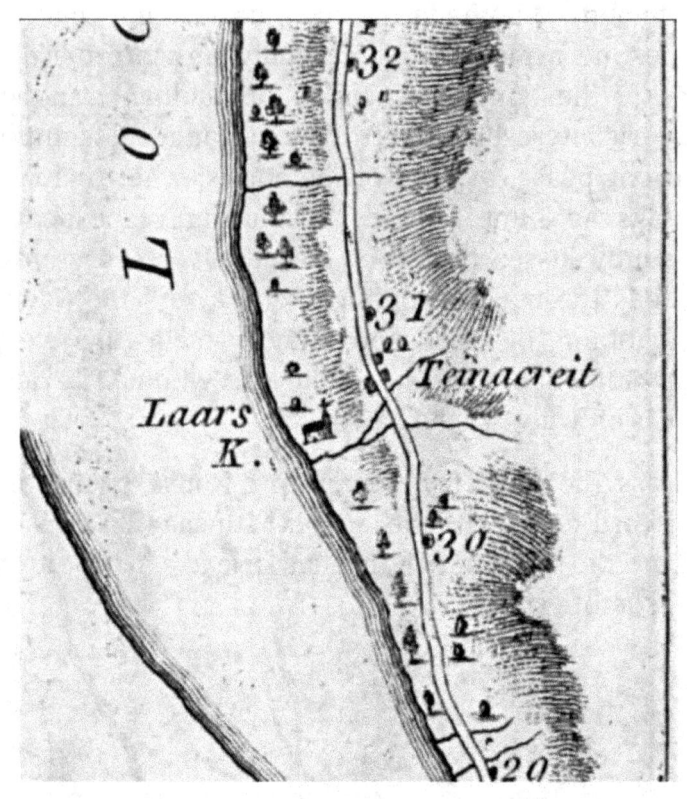

Lawers
From Taylor and Skinner's Survey of Scottish Roads 1776

Appendix G

Lawers –

The Oldest Known Photograph

This recently discovered photograph of Lawers has lain unseen for 100 years; and is the oldest known picture of the abandoned village. Taken from the waters of Loch Tay, looking north, the photograph probably forms part of the innovative work undertaken by the Glasgow Photographic Society and The Photographic Society of Scotland, during the period *1852 – 1864*. Providing us with answers to several key questions regarding Lawers, the importance of this image cannot be overstated.

The large house in the centre of the photograph is the House of Lawers, home to the Lady of Lawers. The picture plainly shows both sides of the property were a two-storey dwelling.

It was previously thought that only the eastern portion (the right-hand side) of the structure was inhabited by the Lady, as there is no obvious internal doorway now visible between the two sides of the house. However, this photograph clearly shows that, not only were both sections of the building two storeys in height; but were obviously built simultaneously, forming one residence. The western section (as mentioned earlier in the book) appears to possess thicker walls and could therefore have formed part of the original outer walls of the castle or tower house that occupied the site prior to 1645. Ironically, despite having much thicker walls, the western portion of the property has deteriorated to a much greater extent. Following the Lady's death, the house become the Milton of Lawers farmhouse. It is probable that the house was divided into two at this point, with the western half becoming a cattle byre and store house.

It is most likely that the Lady required a larger property for herself, her husband, guardians, and perhaps a servant or two. Whatever the original layout of the building, this photograph offers more clues into the Lady's living arrangements than has previously been possible. Also note the open aspect to the front, affording the occupants an unobstructed view of Loch Tay. Photographs taken later, during the Edwardian era, show a substantial growth of trees in front of the house. However, in this image, the land between the house and the loch is still relatively clear.

Interesting, the large-windowed, southern frontage to the church, overlooking the loch, appears to have been harled, then painted white. This was not previously known and is not apparent in any other known images of the building. The treatment was, and is, still commonplace, providing protection against the harsh and wet climate. Similar examples can be observed on the nearby churches at Killin and Kenmore.

However, perhaps most intriguingly of all, is the presence of the stone wall in the foreground. This wall no longer exists in this form; but its positioning in this photograph matches my estimate for the original castle boundary wall. It also formed the retaining wall for the path leading down to the pier and as some protection against high water levels in the loch.

Although the majority of the stones still survive, albeit it, in a tumbled down state, this photograph clearly shows they were part of a once much higher wall, probably that of the original castle. Perhaps, then, part of the castle's outer wall still remained intact at the time this photograph was taken? My assertion, earlier in the book, regarding the position of the original structure, seems to be supported by this image, particularly as it is almost certain that the castle would have occupied this most advantageous of strategic positions, bordering the two footpaths into the village, and with a commanding vista of Loch Tay.

Appendix H

The Lady, the Loch, and the Weather

Of the many prophecies attributed to the Lady of Lawers, two notable themes emerge – her antipathy towards the growing wealth of the Campbells, and her respect for the ominous power of the Loch and the Highland weather. Both points undoubtedly mirror the day-to-day concerns of those living among the scattered communities nestled along the shores of the Loch.

Four centuries ago, with no scientific method of forecasting or explaining the unpredictable nature of the storms, it is perhaps not surprising that folklore, legend, and weather are inextricably intertwined.

The Lady no doubt saw the broody storms and mysterious changes in Loch Tay's moods as either indicators of malevolent spirits, or as a precursor to some dreadful event. Her foresight regarding the loss of the ridging stones bound for Lawers Church, and her prophecy concerning the land freezing and being 'laid waste for seven miles', seem to indicate a fear and respect for the power of the weather. Perhaps, in predicting this wintry event, she may have foreseen the only two recorded instances in history - 1771 and 1785 – when Loch Tay completely froze over. On the final occasion, two men actually crossed the ice on foot, by first taking the precaution of pushing a boat ahead of them.

One of The Lady's seemingly unfulfilled predictions relates to a 'great loss of life' caused by the sinking of the ship on Loch Tay.

More than a century before the arrival of The Lady at Lawers, a similar tragedy had already occurred, the tale of which she no doubt became familiar with.

At Lagfearn, halfway between Fearnan and Lawers, there is a rough stone slab with a simple cross carved on it. According to tradition, a market was once held there, until one day, a heavily laden boat, was returning from the market towards the south side of the Loch. Sadly, all the occupants were drowned in a tragedy which became known as 'The Drowning of Lawers.' To avert any such accidents in the future, the market was moved eastward to Inchadney.

Perhaps The Lady's fear of such a watery catastrophe was also related to the mysterious, unpredictable, and (to a seventeenth century mind) entirely unfathomable phenomenon which occasionally occurred on Loch Tay.

To those living in close proximity to the waters of the loch, the following spectacle, which was first recorded in 1784, and then again in 1794, must have seemed like the work of some mystical force.

Local recollections of the events of 1784 were researched and then recorded by Rev. Dr Marshall in his 1879 book *Historic Scenes in Perthshire*:

"While we are on Loch Tay we may notice a singular phenomenon which it has occasionally exhibited. Its waters have been strangely and strongly agitated. This

has occurred in the calmest of weather, and without visible local cause whatsoever; the presumption, therefore, being, that the phenomenon is ascribed some commotion deep down in the bowels of the earth. The most violent of the agitations to which we refer took place on the 12th September, 1784, beginning about nine o'clock in the morning. On tbe south side of the village of Kenmore is a bay of the loch, 460 yards long, and 200 broad, and averaging from two to three feet in depth. The water of that bay suddenly retired about five yards from its ordinary boundary, and in four or five minutes flowed out again. For a quarter of an hour it thus ebbed and flowed three or four times.. Then, all at once, the water left for a distance of ninety to a hundred yards, leaving the bottom of the bay dry, and rushed northwards, raised by conflicting currents into a wave five or six feet high. This wave, on reaching the depth of the Loch, rolled westward, gradually subsiding till, in about five minutes, it disappeared, and the whole expanse of the water returned to its ordinary level. During this time, the river, which leaves the loch on the north side of the village, was observed flowing backwards; the weeds at the bottom which before pointed in the usual direction of the stream, were turned the contrary way; and the channel of the river was left dry for about twelve feet on each side. Under the bridge, which is about seventy yards from the lake, the stream completely failed in places where there had previously been a depth of eighteen inches of water.

Nothing particular was observed in the state of the atmosphere this time. The weather was perfectly calm; and it could barely be perceived that the motion of the clouds was from the north-east. Nor could it be ascertained that any sensible motion of the earth was felt in the neighbourhood. On the five succeeding days an ebbing and flowing was observed, about the same time of the morning, and of nearly the same duration, but by no means to the same extent as on the first day."

Barthélemy Faujas de Saint-Fond, an eminent French geologist, visited Kenmore shortly after this unusual event and became hugely interested in the matter, estimating that the waters had receded a total of 152 feet from the banks of Loch Tay. He left an extremely detailed account of these conclusions in his 1799 study *Travels in England, Scotland, and the Hebrides: Undertaken for the Purpose of Examining the State of the Arts, the Sciences, Natural History and Manners, in Great Britain.*

Sir Archibald Geikie edited Saint Fond's book in the early twentieth century, commenting that, *"such occillations of levels in lakes, now known as seiches, are sometimes caused by subterranean movements, but probably more frequently by the effect of atmospheric disturbances."*

These strange agitations in Loch Tay during 1784 were also witnessed by the minister of Kenmore, Rev. Thomas Fleming,

"On the next, and the four succeeding days. an ebbing and flowing was observed nearly about the same time, and for the same length of time, but not at all in the same degree as on the first day."

His account of the strange events was published in 1788 in the first volume of *The Transactions of the Royal Society of Edinburgh*, and in *The Statistical Account of Scotland, County of Perthshire 1796.*

Rev. Colin Macvean of Kenmore onserved the strange disturbance which occurred on Loch Tay on July 13th !794, noting that *"Loch Tay experienced similar movements, although not so violent, nor of long continuance."*

In 1994 Dr R.W. Duck, from St Andrews University, was asked to comment on these strange incidents,

"A possible explanation for these strange water movements is related to the fact that the central portion of Loch Tay. between Fearnan and Ardeonaig. is developed along the line of a major. north-east to south-west trending geological fracture known as the Loch Tay Fault. This feature can be traced from Glen Tilt in Highland Perthshire southwards to beneath the southern end of Loch Lubnaig in the Trossachs. The deepest part of Loch Tay (161 m) is located directly above this fault, where the bed is a remarkable 55 metres below sea level.

While one cannot be certain, there is a strong possiblity that the cause of Loch Tay's strange ebbings and flowings in the eighteenth century was due to small but sudden earth movements on the Loch Tay fault plane."

Thankfully, the strange geological sensation, which had been known to rattle windows in Killin, Lawers, and Kenmore, has not been recorded for at least seventy years.

Perhaps the Lady of Lawers possessed a unique insight into the strange and unpredictable behaviour of the Loch, which can only now be explained, thanks to our modern level of scientific understanding.

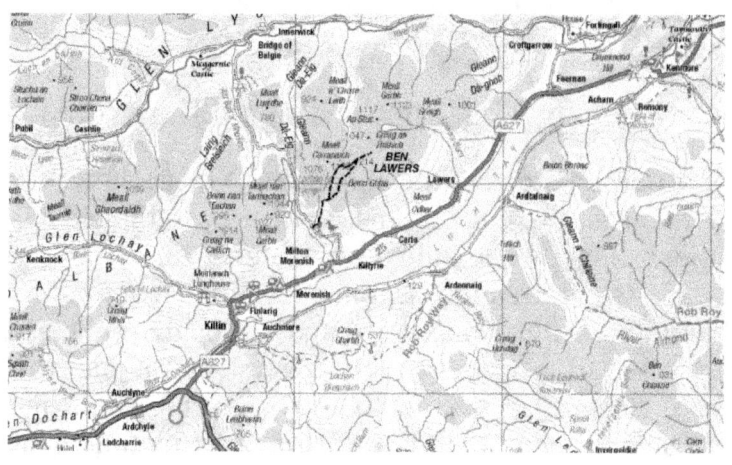

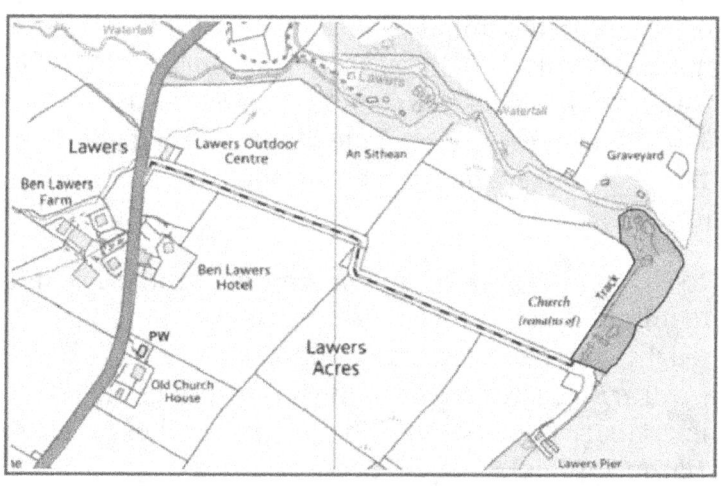

Visiting The 'Lost' Village of Lawers

It is possible to visit the abandoned village, however there are no road signs and the settlement is approximately one mile down a steep track from the road. Its charm and unspoiled nature are due to the unique location and untouched atmosphere. Please treat the site with respect, take your litter home with you, close all gates behind you; leaving this time capsule as you found it. There are no toilets or facilities at the site.

Travelling between Kenmore and Killin on the A827, you will reach the village of Lawers after approximately 7 miles. The track to the old village is approximately 400 metres after the Horn Carvers, on the left-hand side, between Caochan House and the Ben Lawers Hotel. Post code PH15 2PA. Please note, there is no direct bus or train service operating in the area.

Do NOT attempt to take your car down the track, it is unsuitable for vehicles. There is limited parking nearby, however you may be able to park at the hotel, if you are a customer, or in the large yard of the house next door, marked 'Parking for hillwalkers' (small charge applies).

Please park with consideration and remember the track is steep, and unfortunately is not suitable for wheelchairs. Please take care, when exploring the remains, due to the large number of fallen stones and heavy undergrowth in places.

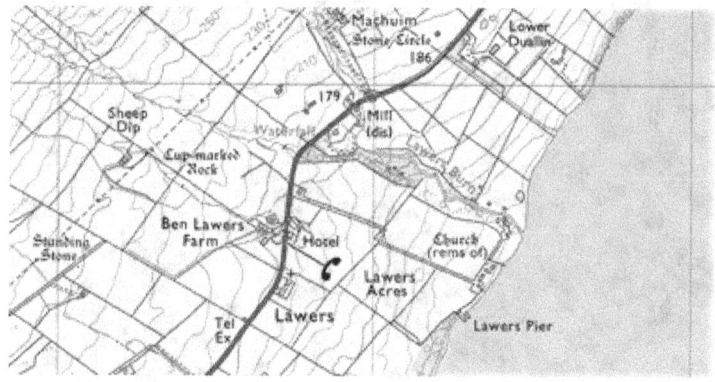

Entering the Old Village

At the bottom of the track, enter through the gate in front of you.

Ahead of you, and to the right, are the remains of the Ferryman's cottage and the pier. Ahead of you and to your left are the two-storey remains of the Lady of Lawers' house, one other cottage and the church. In the tumbledown doorway to the church (facing south) you may be able to see the date stone, inscribed 1669, lying on the floor. On the east side of the church, witness the huge tree which has grown into the building and now towers over the remains. Perhaps this is the legendary tree predicted to grow from the grave of the Lady of Lawers?

The bridge across Lawers Burn

From the church, head to your right (east) through the gate into the open field. (This was once a cobbled street linking the two parts of the village. It is still possible to pick up pieces of cobbled stone lying on the grass). After approximately 100 metres you will reach the second part of the village, built around 1752 and just after. There are remains of several cottages, a lime kiln, and outbuildings, surrounding common ground. The remains of fireplaces can still be seen within the ruins.

Across the wooden bridge is the Cladh Machuim graveyard, which is accessed by ingeniously designed steps built into the surrounding wall.

I hope you enjoy your journey back in time and can forget the hectic nature of the modern world for a moment . . .

To see the scale model of the old village of Lawers and some interactive information boards prepared by the author, please pay a visit to the Breadalbane Reading Room in Kenmore (next to the Taymouth Castle arch). Check their Facebook page for opening hours

To keep yourself updated on the conservation and protection of this precious historical site, please visit:

https://www.oldlawersvillage.co.uk/

Acknowledgements

The following people, journals, books, newspapers and websites have made this publication possible, and I am indebted to them for their help, for the information supplied, and for their permission to reproduce photographs. Other photographs within the book fall under the public domain, or the original copyright is unknown.

Kay Liney, Aberfeldy Museum, Wikipedia, for maps provided with the courtesy of National Library of Scotland, Kelso Cathedral, *Survivals in Belief Among the Celts*, by George Henderson, *'In Famed Breadalbane'* by the Rev Gillies, *Superstitions of the Highlands & Islands of Scotland* by John G. Campbell, Clan Campbell, Dundee Courier, British Newspaper Archive, The Scotsman, *Surviving In The Shadows* by Mark Bridgeman, Perthshire Advertiser, Michael Haigh, Alexa Reid, Fearnan Village Association, Clan MacFarlane, Windhill Origins, Scots Magazine, Gaelic Myth & Legend, *The Highland Tay* by Rev. Hugh MacMillan, University of Edinburgh, The New Statistical Account of Scotland (1833-1845), University of Glasgow, Bens Lawers Historic Landscape Project, Neil Hooper and Andrew Warwick, Dundee Advertiser, Canmore, National Records of Scotland, The Martintown Mill Preservation Society Ontario, Commonwealth War Graves Commission, Kenmore Church. *The Highland Clans of Scotland (1923)*, by George Eyre-Todd and The Keepsake 1837. Laura L. McNeal. Hugh Purvis, Killin Past and Present History Group.

The Author

Mark Bridgeman lives in Aberfeldy and maintains a passion for local history. His other titles are available from The Watermill Bookshop, Aberfeldy, The Highland Bookshop, Fort William, Adventure Into Books, Blairgowrie, Waterstones, and amazon.co.uk.

The River Runs Red
Nineteen true stories of murder, mystery and deception from Highland Perthshire's dark past. Read about one of Scotland's most infamous murders and the psychic who located a body.

Blood Beneath Ben Nevis
21 true stories of murder, myth and mystery from Fort William and Lochaber, covering the years 1700 – 1971.

Learn about the massacre in a cave, ghosts in the High Street and take part in a £10 million treasure hunt!

Surviving In The Shadows
The surprising story of cricket in Highland Perthshire, from 1850 to the present day. Read about Breadalbane Cricket Club's links to test cricket and some of the biggest names in the history of the game.

Footsteps at Finlarig
The story of Killin's hidden castle, its many famous visitors, its literary connections and its unique place in the history of Scotland.

The Dark Side of the Dales
True stories of murder and mystery and robbery from the Yorkshire Dales, including new evidence in two unsolved murders.

Perthshire's Pound of Flesh
True stories of revenge and retribution from Perthshire's dark past. Perth Waterstones' Book of the Year 2023.

The Nearly Man
The remarkable true story of one man's incredible life, encompassing some of the most traumatic events of the 20th-century. An unbelievable read.

Blood Across The Water
More stories of murder and mystery from the Highlands and Islands. A sequel to Blood Beneath Ben Nevis.

The Scottish Murder Book
Fourteen sensational murder trials from the High Court in Perth. Featuring cases from Perthshire, Angus, and Fife.

For further stories and news follow Mark @:

www.facebook.com/markbridgemanauthor/
www.markbridgemanauthor.co.uk
instagram @markbridgemanauthor
X @markbridgemanauthor
threads: @markbridgemanauthor

Brindle Books Ltd

We hope that you have enjoyed this book. To find out more about Brindle Books Ltd, including news of new releases, please visit our website:

https://www.brindlebooks.co.uk

Please feel free to contact us should you have any queries, and you can let us know if you would like email updates of news and new releases. We promise that we won't spam you with lots of sales emails, and we will never sell or give your contact details to any third party.

Our email address is:
contact@brindlebooks.co.uk

If you purchased this book online, please consider leaving an honest review on the site from which you purchased it. Your feedback is important to us, and may influence future releases from our company.

To view our current releases, please scan the QR code below:

www.ingramcontent.com/pod-product-compliance
Lightning Source LLC
Chambersburg PA
CBHW050236120526
44590CB00016B/2114